RUN/STOP-RESTORE:
10TH ANNIVERSARY EDITION

LENARD R. ROACH

authorHOUSE®

AuthorHouse™
1663 Liberty Drive
Bloomington, IN 47403
www.authorhouse.com
Phone: 1-800-839-8640

First published by AuthorHouse 3/09/2011

ISBN: 978-1-4567-1922-7 (e)
ISBN: 978-1-4567-1923-4 (hbk)
ISBN: 978-1-4567-1924-1 (sc)

Library of Congress Control Number: 2011900283

Printed in the United States of America

Any people depicted in stock imagery provided by Thinkstock are models, and such images are being used for illustrative purposes only. Certain stock imagery © Thinkstock.

This book is printed on acid-free paper.

ACKNOWLEDGEMENTS –

I would like to thank the following people and organizations for their help in getting the book compiled:

My wonderful family and friends for their constant support and occasional kick in the butt to get me on track to get this project done;

The Commodore Users Group of Kansas City, Inc. for their help in deferring some of the cost it took to make this second volume a reality;

The Fresno Commodore Users Group for their contributions to the work;

And finally to Juli Zuel, whose husband Carl introduced me to the Commodore machine in the first place and without his training I would not be apt to use the machine like I do now. Like all students, I seek to surpass the master, but nobody could beat his skill on the keyboard. God bless you, Hunter and Julianna.

CONTENTS

INTRODUCTION

It was ten years ago that inspiration hit me from above like a stray bowling pin and brought me to create a collage of some of my best articles I have written and post them in book form, with introductions and illustrations, and print the whole thing using the greatest computer of all time – the Commodore 64/128. This book, named after a Commodore command, has long since been out of print – until now.

Presenting a newly revised version of a great Commodore classic sure to stir up those memories of nostalgia within those who remember the days when BASIC was da bomb and bulletin board systems were the way to make electronic communication with fellow computers users a reality.

This edition is not just a re-print of what has already been done, but an updated version complete with:

NEW FACADES – Each story contains a new introduction viewing each article from a fresh perspective adding to the text the ten years of time and great 20/20 hindsight on the Commodore for the 21st century.

NEW STORIES – Five new stories that have only been previously released in local, national, and international Commodore newsletters and magazines have been added, each with their own façade, to give this tenth anniversary edition a fresh pizzazz never seen in any Commodore book of its kind.

A FRESH LOOK – Run/Stop-Restore: 10th Anniversary Edition has been washed, dried, and fluff folded using a whole new blend of imagination to give the book a fresh, clean look and feel, making this edition a great read and helps avoid any form of rash when you hold the cover.

Why now? Why wait ten years to re-create this volume of Commodore literature and not some other time in the past? My reasoning is simple: I have been steadily writing for Commodore newsletters over the last ten years and was hoping to create a completely different volume of

Commodore work, but when it was brought to my attention that the only copy left in my possession of Run/Stop-Restore was one autographed to my wife, I was ready to make more and present them to the Commodore community at large as a reissue. At first I was going to just re-copy the pages from the master manuscript and re-bind the work for sale, but when I went over the pages, I saw that I needed to jazz up the work a little. Also, I have written some interesting material over the last ten years that would probably interest the rest of the retro-computer users of today, so I started the task of placing all those articles together and, instead of making a new book, merged some of my earliest work with the works done today. This will also give you, the reader, a chance to see how I have graduated from the writer I was ten years ago, to the writer I am now. In short, this volume is a compilation of my best work over the last decade and a half of writing about the Commodore computer and some of my adventures I have had with the machine in the way of working on programs and writing articles and stories based on it.

Commodore has been nothing but fun for me over the last twenty total years. Even though I came on late in the Commodore game, I still was able to find enough support and material to make use of the machine for the time before Commodore went "underground," as I would put it. Used basically as a writing machine, I got further into Commodore when I started playing games and even later finding game construction kits that would allow even the least in knowledge user to get into the fun and start making things that would set other users on edge. But nothing could top a person's fun by actually getting into the BASIC of Commodore itself and start writing programs on my own from the basement up. Never have I used a more user friendly computer as I have found in Commodore machines. Even though I refer to myself as a "shade tree programmer," some of the things I type into memory often come up as something someone could use to make life easier or just simply show a different way to approach the machine. I have been called a "cave dweller" by some since I use so little of any of the new machines and when I do, my knowledge of such machines make me look like a kindergartener in comparison to those who can breeze through an IBM like it was made of yogurt. Sometimes I think about it and I decide that I don't care what others may think. I proudly wear the badge of a Commodore user, but I also bend a little backwards and allow those who have a differing of opinions about the machine to speak their minds. I get laughed at sometimes in social gatherings when people learn that I use what they may call "archaic" computer machinery, but little do they realize that what they basically have now in the way of hardware and software for the up to the minute computer, was first realized and successfully executed on a Commodore unit. Commodore, in my opinion, simply passed the torch on to other formats so they could develop into bigger and better machines than what the Commodore is. But one should never forget one's roots, and by putting some of the things I have done and experienced into print is my contribution to making this possible.

I hope not only to draw a former user back into the good old days when Commodore reigned as king, but also introduce younger, more adept users to the world of what Commodore represents to the computer world both then and now. I tried my best to avoid writing another history book of what Commodore is and how it works, but more of an "experience" book, taking you on a journey with me back to the past when Commodore was boss, and bring you to the present with new things coming out for the machine, especially those things coming from my own warped and crusted mind. I hope to show you what can easily be done on a Commodore with just a few simple commands, proper placement of subroutines, and a lot of GOTO and GOSUB commands.

As you read the forthcoming pages, please enjoy them as they were intended. I write as a user and player of the Commodore, and not just some historian who has been given the assignment of putting together a collection of information and technical data to present in some sort of impersonal facts and figures volume. As a fellow user, I hope that you can capture the challenge and all out fun that Commodore presents through the pages I have written. Commodore came into being when people and computers were learning to work together, before computers became so much a part of our integrated world like they are now.

So no matter your opinion about the Commodore, be it the ghost of a forgone past or still a big part of the future for computers both today and tomorrow, you'll find "Run/Stop-Restore: 10th Anniversary Edition" a book you will want to read again and again just to get that feel of what computing was.

THE NEW FAÇADE TO – "WELCOME TO MY WORLD"

This is a new story added to this edition. This story was first released in the magazine The Interface, the Fresno Commodore Users Group's bi-monthly publication. I have always wanted to make a farce piece about where I lived and this was one of those times where something like this would fit into the world of Commodore. This story takes you through my neighborhood and down the streets to the Roach Hotel which houses the mighty Commodore machine and selected hardware that makes it work. I also go through the personnel and each room of the house nicknamed The Roach Hotel by one of my pastor friends out in Colorado. Many good things have happened to us in this place, as well as much wickedness; but I am guessing that is pretty much what would happen in anybody's home. The hard part I think is to get past all the problems and go into remembering the good stuff and keeping our focus on that. We live in a world where the family unit is slowly starting to erode into something that it was never meant to be and without the family staying together, there will be little hope for a future for our children and our children's children.

But I wisp philosophical and I do apologize for stepping off the path. The point behind this story is to just have fun with the gift of words we all possess and to reveal to the reader what it takes to house the great Commodore machine that has been my electronic friend for almost two decades. When this story was first published I got some great feedback like "I was laughing my head off with every word" to "It makes me glad that I pass through your town on my way to my destination and never stop in." Please enjoy.

WELCOME TO MY WORLD
(A parody)

Hail and well met fellow Commodore users! This time I am going to talk a little about what can be found when you come to visit the Roach Hotel, situated in lovely Kansas City Kansas.

The Roach Hotel sits on Corona in middle downtown Kansas City Kansas. It is a lovely one story building that houses me, my youngest son, one rat, two fish, one dog, and three cats. The dog just recently stopped trying the eat the cats, and the cats just recently stopped trying to eat the fish and rat, so all is harmony when you come for a visit to our little hovel in the Coronado Hills subdivision just off US 24 highway (State Avenue).

The neighbors here at the Roach Hotel are friendly and always glad to hear from you, and they let you know it. Every time my Neon starts at 7:00 am and the alternator belt squeals it's good morning to the neighborhood, everyone comes out to say hello. However, I don't think that "Shut that d—m thing up." Or "Why don't you fix that piece of s—t?" constitutes as a hello, but when it comes to the Hotel, everything is bright and rosy.

As you cruise into Coronado Hills, everybody greets you with a wave. Yet, at some times, I wish they would use all their fingers when they wave. However, they are kind enough to let you know that you are number one by extending the longest digit of the hand to you. Such great people live here near the Hotel, and there is always a cheery hello that comes from all of them in the form of "F—k you, cracka!"

As you enter the hotel, you enter the lounging room, complete with our large in a wooden box 26 inch television complete with some of the best cartoon shows and movies on DVD like The Incredulous, Dora the Exploder, and Ice Aged. On top of the entertainment complex is where Sable, the guard rat keeps an eye on each person entering the Hotel, wondering what each of you would be like for dinner. Don't worry, however, she is harmless – sometimes. Next to her near the closet door are the dragon fish Spike, and the picosamus Zoom. They like to be fed promptly at 7:00 am, and they will just about eat anything – fish food, tin cans, fingers – whatever they can get a hold of.

A turn to the right and you have our lounging chair – one sofa, one loveseat, and one recliner, or the "Command Chair" as I put it. Everyone is welcome to sit and enjoy themselves while they wait on whatever it is they are waiting on – dinner, a snack, or an escape plan out of there. In the command chair is where I do most of the work when it comes to putting things onto computer as the Hotel has, not one, not two, but THREE computers that are all tied together by a router found in one of the rooms.

About eight steps to the west and a turn to the south you will find yourself in the kitchen/laundry room. Here is where the great meals consisting of Hamburger and Tuna Helpers are concocted and set before you to enjoy or feed to the fish at your leisure. A few steps into the kitchen and a turn to the left puts you into the back of the Hotel where the washer and dryer are. Sometimes we get a little absent minded at the Hotel and we either serve your laundry and wash your food, or the other way around. Such is the life as it is in the Hotel.

From the main entrance to the left you find the first door to the left, which is our luxurious bathroom, decorated in a seaside setting. Here is where our guests shower, shave and poo, whichever the case may be. Towels are plentiful in the towel closet at the end of the hall, but be sure to get your towel before you get ready for your bath, or else you're in for an embarrassing time of it as everyone in the lounging room will be able to see everything whole and natural, just as the good Lord made you.

One thing I must mention about the loo: On the back of it is a beautiful sculpture of dolphins playing in the surf that comes with built in sound. As you rise from completing your business, the dolphins made a playful noise of clicks and chirps while water flows from the top of the sculpture, congratulating you on a successful trip. Just one of the extras you will find when your visit the Roach Hotel.

As you head down to the end of the hall you come to one of our great rooms in the Hotel. This one is occupied by our resident technician, mechanic, all around fixit guy, and my son, Gabriel. He works hard to make sure all the computers and household items, as well as vehicles, work to top mechanical performance. His bed takes up over eighty percent of his room, making closet access and access to his desktop computer, which houses also the router and wireless printer I must add, a little difficult but even though Gabe is six feet six, he moves around that room like a cat.

A half step out of his room to the west and a head turn to the left you will find where I, the great and mighty, omnipotent, stomper and poobah of newsletter writing and editing hang my hat. My room is larger than Gabe's, so I get to house more stuff like a dresser, a china cabinet (which I use for a work clothes cabinet) a queen size bed, and my wife's vanity table. These chambers are off limits to all guests except those invited in, and that is only for an open door visit, so don't get any silly ideas!

Another full step to the west and another turn of the head to the left and you will come across the pride and joy of the Roach Hotel – the computer room. Here is where the great Commodore 128 sits on a large desk facing the west wall. Out of this room come such great writings as The Interface, Ryte Bytes, books, plays, and other miscellaneous trinkets that happen to come in my head. This room is open to everyone who is interested in using a Commodore computer.

So where do guests sleep? Well, if you're adventurous – and I know you are – you can stretch out in our lounging area in sleeping bags, or blankets that can be provided by the Hotel. If you don't mind being used as a raceway for the cats during their midnight rampage through the Hotel, you can get a decent night's sleep and wake up stiff and tired and ready for day of fun at the Hotel.

What do we do for fun here at the Roach Hotel? If you are game, you can stroll in our somewhat well kept back yard that views all the neighbor houses, but be careful of the recycled Alpo piles that dot the yard. We use these for fertilizer to make sure that the Hotel's grass is green and lush each spring after the winter thaw. Out the front door, you can always play the never ending game of "Dodge the Drunk Driver" or run with the game of "Escape the Rabid Dog." For those wishing to venture off property kevlar, flak jackets, and M-16s will be issued free of charge by Hotel staff.

From what I have described you can already tell it's nothing but non-stop fun and adventure at the Roach Hotel, so be sure to book your visit with us soon. Our phone number can be found on most of the bathrooms walls around some of the biggest name truck stops of the country.

We look forward to meeting you!

THE NEW FAÇADE TO—
"MY PERSONAL HISTORY
WITH THE COMMODORE"

As I was going over this entry to the book, I was looking at all of the grammatical and spelling errors that I committed during its writing that sneaked into the first edition. As you read it, I hope you get to see a cleaner, more readable article.

Reading this piece again brought back memories that I had almost forgotten. Carl, the man mentioned at the beginning, has been gone for almost twenty years. He died early in one of those "not fair" situations of life that seems to rear its ugly head from time to time, claiming the lives of good people, while unscrupulous people seem to live long, get wealthy, and cheat their way into a distant grave. Carl left behind a beautiful wife and two children, both of whom should be about in their early to late teens by the printing of this edition. I hear nothing from his widow or his parents anymore, so I always pray that all are doing well, in good health, and prospering.

Getting into Commodore was one of those brilliant moves that, if it were done earlier in my career, would have been much more beneficial then back in 1988 when I finally jumped into the game. Back then, when Commodore clubs were more plentiful, it would have been of much greater help reach out with the Commodore writings and Commodore products that I had worked on much later, than now, but I have been told time and time again, "to everything there is a season, and for everything a time and purpose under heaven." There was a good reason for me to enter into the Commodore realm when I did, and I am thinking that one of those reasons was to get me back behind a keyboard, changing from a typewriter to a computer, and into the world of writing. Even programs fall into the writing genre since each piece of code has to be typed in some form of funky English that only can be understood by anther coder and the Commodore computer. Believe it or not, I got into programming the Commodore because I liked writing the directions on how to use my programs. I talk more about programming in a later chapter.

MY PERSONAL HISTORY
WITH THE COMMODORE

I met my first Commodore Business Machine in 1982. My best friend Carl got a Commodore 64 and 1541 disk drive for his seventeenth birthday at the cost to his parents of $850. It was cool - all the colors, the games, and you could use your television with it, just like the Atari 2600 game system, but like an ass head I looked down on it. It wasn't "for me" - I was raised under the old school of the "if it works, don't fix it" philosophies. My pen and stacks of blank writing paper has worked in the past and it'll still work today; so I walked away from what would soon become my future.

When my buddy graduated in 1983, he quickly applied at Wichita State University, was accepted, and for the next nine years he and his Commodore 64 (which expanded to a Commodore 128 while there) and 1541 disk drive (which transformed into a 1571) got an education. In Wichita, he joined the Kappa Sigma fraternity, where he became quickly known as the only man with an on-site computer at any frat house on campus. Anything a fraternity brother needed to know, Carl was the man who got on-line and checked the local boards and GEnie, and found the tidbit of information the brother needed.

I came to Wichita one day on business in 1986, and detoured myself to the WSU campus to check on him and his welfare. I saw the Commodore 128, I saw what he was doing with it, and I was hooked. I wanted in on this computer business stuff - real bad. What finally sold me on getting a Commodore computer was the game entitled "The Incredible Hulk." I stayed in his room playing that game all night while he slept, but I never solved it.

For the next twelve months I looked for a Commodore 64 and disk drive but everything was too pricy for a man who made $13,000 a year. I was hurt, but I carried on in my quest.

Then on Christmas of 1987, I got a present from my wife's best friend that was in the shape of a Commodore 64 and tape drive. I went nuts!! I immediately went to Wichita before the year's end and Carl got on-line for me and downloaded a copy of Speedscript 3.0. That's all I needed - I spent two years writing on Speedscript all my material. I got a modem from my son for my birthday the following year and began entering the world of cyberspace at the breakneck speed of 300 bps.

As time continued to march forward I increased in Commodore knowledge and equipment. I wore out my Commodore 64 and upgraded to a Commodore 128. My wife, for another Christmas, got me a 1541 II disk drive, which I still have and use today. It's about seven years old and I know that the Commodore Man has rebuilt it at least three times.

During the early '90s, I made two crowning achievements in the Commodore computing universe -- I submitted and published my first real programming attempt called "Check It Out," which appeared in the November/December 1992 issue of RUN magazine. I was now a professional computer programmer and writer. Also, I stepped out on my own and opened my first and only BBS, "The Pulpit." I had a Commodore 128, Ivory BBS v3.3 and four 1541s for start up. During its one year run my wife went to Sgt. Butch of the KBPD BBS in Belton, Missouri, and made a bid on dismantling and buying all his Commodore software and hardware. For the total cost of an Amiga 1000, Amiga 500, two 1541s, three 1571s, a 1581, a HD-100 hard drive, three monitors (two 40/80s and a 40 column), three Commodore 128 (two with JiffyDOS) and two Commodore 64s, along with C*Base 3.0 and C*Base 2.0, and acres and acres of software, my wife paid $500. It took two maxi-van loads to haul all that stuff from Belton, Missouri, to Kansas City, Kansas. I eventually sold half the software to the Commodore Man, sold a Commodore 64 to a friend's mother for a word processor, and gave two complete Commodore 128 systems away as Christmas gifts. I sold the Amiga 500 to a user of the Pulpit. I merged the rest of the KBPD's inventory with the Pulpit and for the remaining six months of my BBS' life I ran a large BBS setup. But the cost of running a bulletin board system caught up with me so I dropped the project and shelved the files where they now sit to this day. It also contributed to the demise when the local electric company sent a man with a law enforcement official out to my home to investigate as to why I had such a binge of electrical consumption. They were kind enough to explain that sometimes unscrupulous people grew illegal substance in their homes and the surge of power was their attempt to create an artificial climate to make the necessary vegetation grow properly. I let them examine my home and showed them that I was running a bulletin board system from here and this was where the extra power was going. Needless to say they apologized and left my home dignified, but embarrassed.

In October of 1994, I was introduced to the Commodore User's Group. A bunch of whacked out computer users who were avid about the Commodore computer. These folk were the exact group I was looking for, so in January of 1995, I signed on. It was the best move I ever made for my Commodore and me. From this club I've learned that even though support from public sources was failing there was still help out there for the Commodore. To this day I always turn to the users group for help, repair/replacement of equipment, and advice.

As I sit here today and I look back on the past, I have come to the conclusion that Commodores are best described by me as the "poor man's computer." And if any of you are like me, you're so poor you can't afford a free lunch. I like to stress to computer shoppers that if you need a computer but can't afford the latest IBM or Macintosh, consider a Commodore. My best calculations say that a full Commodore set up costs about 1/10th the price of an IBM or Mac and still accomplish the same tasks to an acceptable degree. I also would like to point out that since Commodore can only extract text from the Internet and the World Wide Web, no nasty pictures can enter into the hands of young children or curious teenagers. Repairs and replacement parts for the Commodore are relatively inexpensive and mostly easy to come by. I try to encourage people who are about to trash their Commodores to make room for an upgrade, to bring the unit to our users group meeting for our team to look at and possibly purchase. Commodore, in my opinion, is the best computer ever made by men. It's a shame that at Commodore's prime, the executives of the time didn't take the lead and make it the mainstream of computers like IBM is today.

With all this need for faster processors and more memory, it makes me wonder when this computer upgrade madness will end. At the same time, it pleases me that though Commodore uses only 64K or 128K of memory at 2mhz of speed, it gives me a proper chance to do my work right and right the first time. Remember, it's not how much memory you have, it's what you do with what you got that counts. In my ten years of using Commodore, I've never seen so many imaginative people make such a small space memory do so much, and the list still grows.

THE NEW FAÇADE TO – "I'LL NEVER TOUCH YOUR COMMODORE AGAIN!"

My wife is a wonderful creation of God – she has tenderness and concern that would make any man happy and I am glad that she chose me to give all that kindness to for the rest of our lives together. Even with the troubles we have had in the past, she was still able to maintain her poise and dignity in the face of the most fierce of adversity. The upcoming story on the next page is a great example of what she can do when she has to deal with such a problem and the problem maker, which in this case, is me.

Please read this piece slowly and see how she handles me in the situation described and with the fewest words possible, makes me look like the fool I was. She was only trying to help and I bit her head off for it. Some things are not worth fighting over and the Commodore is definitely one on those things.

By the time this edition of Run/Stop- Restore gets to the publisher, Alana and I would have been married for twenty seven years. She has put up with my working ungodly hours, being obsessed with project after project, my blowing off dates with her just so I can grab an extra hour or two at work, going to sleep on her while she is trying to have a heart to heart conversation, and a host of other sins that were born in the pit of hell, and yet she still stayed by my side being the faithful woman she has always been. Like most men, I did childish things that I thought at the time were good, well intentioned ideas but in the end it proved to be disastrous, yet she still had the grace and power to stand and patiently wait while the School of Hard Knocks taught me the lessons she already knew and tried to convey to me before the whole ruckus began.

So, here's to that great woman that lives in most men's lives. May she always hold a high pedestal in our hearts forever.

"I'LL NEVER TOUCH YOUR COMMODORE AGAIN!"

Some days are just like others and then you have days that change the course of computing history forever. You wonder if there is any chance of correcting the fatal flaw which created the mishap in the first place, and you hope for such an occasion. Such as what happened to me, but thanks to the users of the Pulpit, this has now changed.

I happened one day not too long after we got our first Commodore in the house. We were short a disk drive so the tape drive provided would have to suffice. Since there was no tape drive material provided for the last ten years or so, we were stuck typing in programs listed in various Commodore magazines that were available at the local bookstore. This was a pain for a while until a system was found that made things a little easier.

The lovely Mrs. Roach was a cashier for about two years before I met her. Thusly, she had ten-key talents that were unsurpassed by nothing save her beauty. Since most type-in programs were in their own machine language text, all one usually had to do was type in a set of numbers until it was done, save the completed work, then load, run and viola! A program was created and activated. This was my wife's strong point, so strong that it made me look like an amateur in programming. I didn't like that.

When it came to the Commodore I wanted to be the big shot. I, instead of some woman who hates computers to begin with, was making a fool out of me programming-wise. I tried to keep in mind that the person who's doing the work is doing it faster than I ever could, but the steamy head of jealously kept creeping up behind me, whispering to me that this machine was mine and nobody should be able to program like that except me!

Finally after being badgered by the unholy green monster long enough I decided to make which quickly would be known forever as the dumbest mistake in my computing life. I jumped all over my "Baby" and told her how much I hated her typing in programs like that! I spouted that I got this machine and therefore she shouldn't have all the fun. This was about as smart as a bowl of corn flakes. My wife calmly stood up from the keyboard, pushed the chair aside to let herself out, and gave me that glare that said, "You're being as stupid as a box of rocks." She stepped away from the unit, but before she did she looked me square in the eye and said straightway, "I'll never touch your Commodore again," then she walked off.

When Alana makes a proclamation like that she does not fill it full of hot air just to see if it will float, she means it. For days afterward when I got stuck I would ask for her help and she would clearly state flat out that I should do it myself. What then took her a few hours, now took me about a week, therefore new games I wanted from magazines took about a fortnight to three weeks to get done.

This computer drought from the missus lasted about five years. She has worked on the computer at the workplace, but not the best of machines, the Commodore. Even after the start of the Pulpit she refused to get on even though I made her a co-sysop. At that time, I caved in. She was never going to touch my Commodore again.

Then an interesting user came on-line one day. She was strong in an alternative religion that was not far from Christianity, but still misdirected in a few vital points of scriptural doctrine. I told the wife that this new user is making statements that would flip her out, so she read over my shoulder at some of the stuff the users was saying, but still not touching the Commodore just like she vowed.

As time wore on and the Pulpit grew in membership, the troublesome user made one of her most fatal mistakes. She posted something along the lines that Jesus is not enough for salvation. I freaked.

"Honey!" I screamed. "You'd better come here! You got to see this!"

Mrs. Roach trotted into the room with her half-hearted look. She scanned the screen as I scrolled the post past her. Her eyes lit up like a dynamite shack exploded in her head.

"What!" she screamed. "How dare her!! She doesn't know her Bible. Get out of the way!"

She kicked the stool I was sitting on out from under me, causing me to thump on the floor and bounce across the room. I sat there for a moment rubbing my bruised butt while she was bellowing to me on how to call up her account. Once past that obstacle, growling all the way since things took longer on the Commodore than the IBM's at work, she got into the sub board where she read the post. I had the stool put back in place and she was sitting down, typing away in response to the user's blatant remarks. Each time she made a mistake she would fall just shy of cursing herself while pounding on the "DEL" key. When she was done, she saved the message. A satisfied look like the cat swallowing the proverbial goldfish came over her face with the thought that she has once again set someone straight concerning spiritual doctrine. Now it was my turn to speak.

"Got it done?"

"Mm hmm," she cooed.

"How do you feel now?"

"Better."

"You do know that you've touched the Commodore, don't you?"

"Yes," she replied. "I've been doing so for quite a while now."

My jaw dropped.

"Excuse me?"

"I've been playing games and working with Robert on some educational software for quite some time," she confessed.

"But," I retorted, "you said that you'd never touch the Commodore again, even after I begged and pleaded with you to try again you said, 'No.'"

"I know," she said with a giggle. "I liked the idea that you appreciated me after all. You were being a donkey's bunghole that day and I knew it, but I wasn't going to let you get away with that without suffering something for saying what you did to me."

I dropped my shoulders and hung my head in shame.

"You're right," I confessed, "and I'm sorry."

I hate it when she's right! She wears it like a gold necklace for a short while, but then she'll drop the attitude just as quickly as she picked it up -- sometimes. I took her hand and led her to the kitchen table where we both sat down and caught up on where we were in life. This computer thing put a wedge between us for some time. It was one of those things that came into the house that we could not agree on, so we avoided the subject. Now, we can finally talk about it freely.

I learned from that moment that you can learn more about your Commodore without actually using it. If an offer for help comes, accept it. She still even to this day can type in a magazine program faster than anyone I know, and all I do is figure out how to use the programs once they are inputted into memory.

Isn't love grand?

THE NEW FAÇADE TO –
"LET'S GET BACK TO BASICS AGAIN"

I have had a lot of vacations since the time this story was written; some fun vacations and others were honey do vacations. My wife just had major surgery at this time and needed some recovery time, so I took some time off to help out. I was selfish to think that I could get some time on the Commodore computer during this break.

I never got the hang of the discipline I mention at the end of the story. In fact, it took the combined lecturing of two people – my boss and an elderly co-worker – to get me to see that if you can work a little bit at a time on the same project every day, eventually those little times will add up to one big accomplishment. Most of the re-writing done on Run/ Stop-Restore 10th Anniversary Edition was done in the quiet of the early morning after working a sixteen hour shift between two jobs. I never did hours upon hours of work on the re-write, but with the little I did do, over time, became the work you bless me with by reading.

I also mention programming and how much I hate it. Sorry, this is a slight misconception. The only thing I hate about writing programs is the little bug that you can't find for days that sorely retards your progress, and sadly it seems that this little bug shows up in every program you sit down to write on any computer – but oh, the joy on the day when all the little bugs are found and the work that you have pounded your head on a croquet stake, as it were, finally runs the way you have pictured in your mind and it is ready for general release! I look forward to Commodore convention season so I can see what is being done with the Commodore by others, and I can show off some of the things I have been doing over the time since the last convention. It is a great time of fellowship that can only be shared by true retro-programming enthusiasts.

So join the party! The only thing really missing is – you.

LET'S GET DOWN TO
BASICS -- AGAIN!

The more I write programs, the more I come to the same conclusion: I hate writing programs!

Then why do it?

Why not? I've got ideas. Good ideas. At least I think they are. Ideas for programs; programs I hope will change the way the world sees Commodore and the way Commodore users see their machines. I think that is the hope of any programmer, no matter what machine they use. Besides, we all could use some new software once in a while no matter how old our machines are. I'm sure there are some IBM 286 users out there that want something that fits their memory capacity. The same goes for the Commodore 64 and Commodore 128 users.

You have heard some of my complaints about programming before: Copyright disputes, time disputes, family disputes (especially if you have kids); which can sometimes lead to: Anger, depression, therapy. There goes the money for that RAM expansion unit!

Now a new problem has arisen: Procrastination.

I took a week off the beginning of March. The Precious Queen of My Universe had major surgery and needed someone to help her about for a while, but she wouldn't need me all the time, especially with her sister in from Wisconsin helping out as well.

"Now," I thought," I will have time to get some serious work on the Commodore done."

Bzzzzzzzzzz! Wrong!

I still had boys in school which needed to be awakened, fed, clothed, drilled into doing their morning chores, hauled off to their respective schools (the oldest goes to high school in Bethel, Kansas; and the youngest to elementary school in downtown Kansas City, Kansas. Also one goes one hour earlier than the other!

Next came breakfast for the M.R.S. (My Radiant Sunshine, or "Mrs." for short). Not much cooking since she is a cereal and toast kind of girl; then its dishes and laundry, along with a little housecleaning, then it's time to get the youngest from school. Half days for kindergarteners here in KC - fetch him and bring him home.

No time on the Commodore yet...

It becomes lunchtime; cooking for four (her sister is still here, but she is doing a lot of talking), eat and then clean up.

Next is naptime. I'm exhausted! Kid is on his Nintendo 64 which shares the monitor with my Commodore 128; there's no Commodore time here either. I get one hour of sleep before the wife calls to me and I have to go to Bethel and get the oldest kid. I yawn, stretch, produce a body noise, and leave for Bethel. On the way back, we talk about the day at school, girls, and how many guys got their foreheads rammed into the wall at lunch.

NOTE FOR MEN: If you have a teenage son and they want YOU to rate a girl, then notice the girl in question and give him your opinion. It is your elderly right as a father to look at other women -- for the boy's sake, but be sure to mention that the girl in question cannot measure up to your beauty at home. Confess this both in private as well as in front of the wife. Remember, what goes around comes around. It's up to you whether you have an athletic cup or a coffee cup on when time arrives.

NOW BACK TO YOUR REGULARLY SCHEDULED DRIVEL:

Back at home, it's "who will Daddy be playing with first?" The oldest son, who just had a hard day at school (for a teen, every day is a hard day at school) or the youngest, who has been playing for the last two and a half hours and is oblivious to my existence anyway. I opt for the oldest, who at that precise moment decides to call his friend and tell him about the girl who made dreamy eyes at him today. Back to the youngest, who doesn't want me to join in because I'll mess up his high score. How is it that every time a child sits down to a video game, he always has a best score going on and can't be disturbed?

No time on the Commodore yet....

Wind down time. Stick my nose into the women's conversation. This is like walking into the loin's cage wearing shorts made of sirloin beef. Guess what part of me got chewed off?

Dinner time. Whip up something fresh and fantastic (Ragu, fettuccine, and ground beef topped with mozzarella shredded cheese in a tube, for example) and feed the bunch. They eat, complain about my cooking (but with a smile), then I clean up the dishes. Boys return to various duties (like playing together, after some coaxing from the parents). The oldest makes the youngest cry. I have to play Judge Judy for the rest of the night and find out who's at fault; by this time it's time to pray and thank God for the day (Psalm 118:24 for Bible buffs out there), then bedtime.

And no Commodore time whatsoever...

This was an average day during my vacation. Nothing went exactly like this every day, but the point was that I procrastinated about time on the Commodore. Where? I shouldn't have taken that afternoon nap. I could have avoided the conversations with my wife and her sister (I'm one, though, who's bound to repeat historical mistakes. It's a man thing) and worked on the machine.

What I need is structure. Maybe that's what you need. Try setting a time on the o'clock to sit at your Commodore, and then use the oven timer to pace your time. When the bell goes ding, you're done and you go to something else. I'm going to try that starting today. Sure, this may not happen every day is different, but some time is better than no time -- and I have no time, or so I think.

We'll see...

THE NEW FAÇADE TO— "IN PRAISE OF MY SONS"

One of the good things I found that I enjoy about rewriting is that I get to travel a lot down memory lane. The things I felt when I first wrote about a subject, the feeling I had when I put the same subject into the first edition of Run/Stop-Restore, and the emotions I have now that I am reviewing the material and preparing it for rerelease. Gabriel and Robert have grown up so much since the time this article was first penned that they hardly seem like the two boys I was referring to back in the day. One of the biggest changes not mentioned anywhere is the boys are no more boys but men, men who take the talents first described in the forthcoming piece and made them into both upcoming as well as present careers. Robert can now fix anything he sets his mind to and Gabriel can made any computer of any format practically sit up, beg, roll over, or whatever. The funny thing is, the talents of both men are interchangeable; Gabriel, also, can fix anything and Robert can easily find his way around a software package or computer operating system by a simple point and click of a mouse.

It took a lot of happiness as well as some hardship to get these men to where they are today and most of it was involuntary. For the hardship, I only wish I could have relieved them of the burdens that they carried so they could spend more of their time as boys and not have grown up so fast. As for the happiness, I am thankful that I got to see the smiles and hear the laughter that echoed through the house during the growing up years.

As you ponder the story on the next page, I would suggest you think of that someone or couple of someones that you got to watch grow up, maybe even participate in the process of making them into successful adults, and be thankful that they turned out the way they did. I'm sure that, for the most part, they could have turned out better, but the best of it all is that they definitely could have turned out worse.

IN PRAISE OF MY SONS

For everyone who has read this column for the last few years know about my two boys, Robert and Gabriel. You have known about their antics from putting superhero collecting cards into my 1541, in the hopes of getting the pictures to show up on my monitor, to giving my 1571 a Southern Baptist immersion in skim milk. You also know about their efforts to make my work on the Commodore a lot easier, from cleaning up my stand to blindly fixing my machines when they are broken. For those of you who don't know either one of them, let me tell you a short story on each that happened just recently.

When I got GEOS 128 v2.0 finally started, I, in my ignorance, put some important files in the waste basket icon of the program; files like GEOS 64 and Desktop 128. These came off my System disk. Now a GEOS user would tell me that this is a major/minor problem since I have a Backup System disk provided with the package, but when GEOS from the master disk refused to load, I panicked, grabbed my backup disk, and through a series of hurried yet unknown steps, I messed it up as well. But providence gave me wisdom enough to transfer a copy of Desktop 128 to a couple of work disks, as per the GEOS manual. I could load GEOS from the master disk, but it would ask for Desktop and I would have to insert a work disk then the program would boot up. No problem as long as I had a second disk of anything GEOS in drive #9. This was curious to me, but I let a sleeping dog lie in this matter. I had GEOS running and that was good enough for me.

I did this for about six months until a day came when Gabriel (age 6 at this time) wanted to use GEOPaint. He did everything I showed him to do about disk swapping three or four times to get GEOS to come up, but instead of using the master disk, he used the backup master disk and the main menu was before him without swapping any disks out. He brought this to my attention believing he did something wrong, but when I saw that he used the backup disk, which I believed to be somewhat damaged, I was flabbergasted. How did he do this? Every time I booted the backup disk, the program would loop and reboot until I turned off the Commodore. I had to have him show me what he did. What he did was -- nothing. All he did different was put the backup disk in drive #8 instead of the master disk. GEOS would, upon loading the program from the backup disk, is look for a GEOS formatted disk in drive #9, then continue to load and finally run the program if it found the disk. If not, then the program would loop and load again. I owe a debt of gratitude to my six year old son Gabriel, for getting GEOS 128 to work right even after I messed it up for what I thought was for good.

Now let me tell a story about my oldest son.

Robert (age fourteen at this time) hates my Commodore, basically because it is not an IBM. He wants to play racing games like "Viper" which is only on IBM. I got him "Test Drive" and "The Duel -- Test Drive II" for Commodore. He played them once and then shelved them. In his opinion, those games didn't match up with "Test Drive 4" and "Test Drive 5" on Playstation when it comes to playability and graphics. Now when it comes to getting into the Commodore machinery, he's all gung ho.

One day I was going to make a demo video for a buddy of mine at work, but when it came to running the program, the SID chip only played half the notes to the music I was videotaping. In order for the program to be fully effective, I needed whole sound. I searched by back stock of 64's and 128's and found a keyboard that had a great SID, but something unidentified within the circuit board would only let me run it for five minutes, then the keyboard froze up. Robert had the radical idea of switching out the SID chips, but this meant pulling the chips, a task neither one of us have done before. I've always heard that such work should be done by an experienced computer maintenance repair person and not the home user, but my present usable machine had a bad SID anyway, so I figured we couldn't do any worse to it.

After a call to the Commodore Man to find the location of the SID chip in the 128, we dove in. Cracking the case and removing the heat shield required much undoing of many screws, but soon we were looking at the circuit board of a Commodore 128. Finding chip location U5, Robert took the tongs of a chip puller I had bought recently and gently pried the SID chip out of its location. The thing looked like a rectangular black centipede with silver legs. We did the same for the 128 we were using for parts.

My son then suggested that since we were inside my usable 128, we should take JiffyDOS out of the parting 128 and put it into the 128 we were doing surgery on. Drilling a hole with a punch into the case of the good 128 took some time, but Robert was patient about it. Soon the hole was made and Robert inserted the toggle switch into it, securing it with a flat nut. He grabbed the chip puller again and removed ever so gently the JiffyDOS kernel from the 64 and 128 parts of the 128 and inserted them into the proper chip locations on the repaired 128, making ever so sure that each pin was lined up before it was pressed into place. After we placed the heat shield back on, we set the keyboard back on but did not bolt it down, just in case there was an error, we could get in quickly and change anything out.

Now was the moment of truth -- we reconnected all the serial bus cables and power supply cord. I looked at my son, who stared back at me with unsteady eyes. He knew how much I needed my Commodore to get my work done and I just gave him full trust to operate on its very functioning. If this fails, we were back to square one -- or worse. I gave him a reassuring, confident nod and he flipped the power switch to the "on" position. The red LED on the 128's face came on indicating power, the drives whirred to life, and the basic screen came up on the monitor. I placed my hand on his shoulder; so far, so good. He insisted the he load the music program I wanted to hear, so I let him boot it up. After a short prayer, Robert typed "RUN" and we waited. The Commodore calculated all the data statements and in a very short period of time beautiful, full, harmonious music came flowing out of the speakers. I just about crushed my son with a hug of joy for the fact that both the SID and the JiffyDOS were working perfectly. Our attempt to step out and repair my machine paid off. Rich sound resonated throughout the house and JiffyDOS gave me quick access to everything.

So my deepest gratitude (and possibly a gift or two for each, pending mom's approval) goes to my two sons. Robert, for having the chutzpah to go into the unknown by faith and come out a champion and Gabriel, who in his innocence came up with a better way to deal with an otherwise tedious way to load and run GEOS. These boys are tops in my book.

Upon proofreading the draft of this article, I noticed I mentioned speakers in the plural. This little piece of engineering came from the combined genius of both boys. Robert suggested some time ago to run the sound of Gabriel's Nintendo 64 through the auxiliary ports of my stereo. Robert also found two extra stereo speakers in the basement from an old stereo I had years ago when LP's were still the top thing and merged them with the whole setup. Gabriel suggested I make the Commodore run on all the stereo's speakers, too. With the purchase of four splitters from the discount store and the boy's help, we successfully merged the Nintendo 64's and Commodore's sound system together and ran them through the stereo auxiliary and out through four speakers. With the replacement of the SID chip in my 128, I got deep, resonating bass and sharp, keen high pitches from the tweeters, all in quadraphonic sound.

These boys went from making my Commodore repair guy rich to keeping some of my money in my pocket. Now I can buy some stuff like a 1750 REU and more JiffyDOS chips for my drives. I guess an RS232 wouldn't hurt either. God bless both my sons.

THE NEW FAÇADE TO—
"THE MOST DESTRUCTIVE BABY
IN THE COMMODORE UNIVERSE"

I lost the original publication date to this next story, but according to the piece, it was written around the time my youngest son was one year old, that would put the piece around 1993 or 1994. Since then Gabriel has gone through some very tough but life changing issues. Since then he has gone through and survived leukemia; got to travel to London, England and Churchill, Canada via the Make A Wish Foundation; got his very first job during the difficult economic downturn of 2009; bought his own car and maintained same by his own initiative, along with the help of various individuals that are too numerous to mention.

This next piece almost became a prophecy turned true as Gabriel also learn to repair not only the Commodore computer that still resides on the very same desk mentioned in the story, but also he has learned, through study, trial, and error, how to build a complete IBM system from the ground up. He also knows how to manipulate and maintain both the Windows based software systems most prominent in this day as well as some of the other operating systems existing for other formats. His knowledge for Commodore, however, got lost as the schools of today have opted to put the Windows or Mac OS into the classroom and sadly, he shows no interest in learning the ins, outs, and commands of this dwindling ancient language. But, like most teenagers, he is always on the lookout for the newest, best, and most up-to-date gaming systems or computer software available in the markets.

At the writing of this tenth anniversary edition of Run/Stop-Restore, Gabriel is seventeen and already looking into the local junior college to take classes that will advance him further into his chosen career – whatever that may be. At least he hasn't revealed that information to me.

This story is still dedicated to that great little baby that has now grown into adulthood and is about to spread his wings and try all the things that mom and I have taught him about life and its meaning. Enjoy.

THE MOST DESTRUCTIVE BABY IN
THE COMMODORE UNIVERSE

With the coming of every baby into the world comes the wonders and blessings that the child will provide in the life of every parent; the first coo, the first word, and the first steps, are all exciting things to happen as slowly independence and a new world of exploration opens up. When the child spots your Commodore machine sitting on the computer stand, he then decides that it's time to step out into new horizons never reached before in babydom. Such is the description of my second born. He has already earned the nickname "Tank" for he has single-handedly kept my repair person in business. In fact, I hear that he's going to make the final payment on his Viper this month after I pay for my latest batch of repaired drives, printers, and keyboards.

Basically, this whole wrecking Commodore hardware instilled in my son is my fault. I wanted him to be like his dad and love the Commodore as much as I do. When he was a little past one year, I put a debunked Commodore 64 keyboard into his pen to peck at so he can know the layout before he could comprehended the English language. I hoped by kindergarten he could show his computer prowess by writing, loading, and running his own software before any other kid could figure where the potty was. This was my hope for him, but he much to my chagrin, had other plans.

I quickly forgot that it takes two to make a baby, and in that process some of each parent's genetic code is passed into the child. Well, that part that was declared "Mom's Genetics" came out of him at this time. Mom's first instincts as a little girl was to go behind her dad and remove all the lug nuts from the wheels of any car he happened to be working at his garage after he had just put them on. To disassemble all she touched was her God given mission until she learned through time and error (and a few groundings) not to do that anymore. It took her a few years more to catch on how to reassemble things she took apart. Now she works at a local car dealership tearing up warrantees just like she did her dad's garage years ago.

However, this all comes down to the baby -- the most destructive baby in the Commodore universe. I'm sure we all have our own child horror stories about how the child did something strange to a favorite disk or your Commodore machines. I've heard some doozies but this is a time for me to tell everyone about my son and what he did for me. First of all, let me say that if destroying a computer, let alone a Commodore was to win any awards then I think my son would come out in first place. He's wiped out a lot of machinery and programs quicker than a bad producer can crank out a raunchy "B" horror flick. I think his best act of destruction is when my eldest boy and I were in a mood for a game of computer baseball. We had our ball caps, our peanuts and cracker jacks, and a drive to beat the pants off of each other, but once the disk containing the game program was inserted and the LOAD command given we hit a disk error, and every time we loaded the game, too. After investigation we found a paperclip shoved into the drive that Gabriel later confessed he put there. This, however, did not solve our problems for now the disk was erased, the program gone, and the drive permanently damaged. It required a new drive assembly that costs me a good quarter of a paycheck.

His next feat of annihilation was when I came home with my recently repaired MPS 801 printer, and just as I set it into its place on the computer stand here came Gabriel right behind me and pulled out the command leads from the microprocessor to the print head. From the time he learned to walk and grab he has shoved baseball cards into my 1581, jammed paper clips into my 1541, and changed the face programming of my hard drive to a point where it could not be accessed; but I know that he's only learning. He's discovering the things around him and how they work. He's absorbing data and processing it as only a baby could do. One day all this destroying will prove to be a cornerstone in which he will lean on in the future. One day he just might be the guy to come up with the idea that will show the world that Commodore is still the best home computer in the world and IBM will have to take a back seat.

Don't get me wrong, I love my son. 1541's can be cleaned out, 1581's can have the cards removed, hard drives can be reworked, and 1571's can be replaced, but children cannot. They all are unique works that can baffle even the sharpest programmer. If we all can just take time to show children the right way, then we have done the most difficult programming job all -- shaping the future and making it better for everyone.

This story is dedicated to my youngest son, Gabriel. Keep searching and knowing, you'll find all your answers even at the expense of a few Commodore machines.

THE NEW FAÇADE TO –
"ADD THE FOLLOWING:
3 CATS + 1 COMMODORE = TROUBLE"

Even after ten years between editions, I still love cats. The cats mentioned in this story have long since passed on, but right on schedule, I have acquired three more and for some reason, no matter what, I will always seem to have three cats, no more, and no less, throughout my life. The former location of the Commodore has changed, but these new cats still do the same thing, but this time they try to crawl into places that a mouse couldn't fit into. For example, my new Commodore stand has cabinets and drawers that these cats love to try and crawl into and they can't get enough of hiding from me or each other while at the same time destroying whatever I have stored in the stand, be it disks, mice, or joysticks. They also love to explore what is in the computer closet, where most of my Commodore hardware, software, books, and magazines reside, and they love to just get under foot and try to get my attention away from my Commodore work just enough for me to pet them, or like I say in the upcoming story, just to get noticed. Most of the time these new cats like to walk under the computer chair and tickle the inside of my kneecap with the point of their tails, quickly sending a tickling shock through my system, but most of their fun comes from climbing over the Commodore computer stand, getting in the way of the monitor, or trying their best to make sure they are number one in getting seen, just like the cats before them. I read once that the reason a cat does such antics is because if you don't lock eyes with them upon arrival, they will pester you until you do look at them eye to eye. Once that is done, then the mission, in their furry minds, is complete and they can move on to other things on their agenda. Weird, but loving, my cats are and have always been, retarded.

ADD THE FOLLOWING:
3 CATS + 1 COMMODORE = TROUBLE!

For anyone who has stopped into my place knows that I like cats. They see a lace of fur around every piece of furniture and every knick-knack in the house. You can't keep up with the dusting and cleaning of this menace know to my family as "cat fuzz," so for the most part we leave a small portion of it for either the spring or fall clean up. We honestly thought about waxing the cats, but later decided that this method would make for a group of very naked and ugly cats.

Most people have cats for mouse catching duties but mine are just for looks. I've always had a cat around since my much younger days. My dad always had one on the farm to chase away mice from the goat and chicken sheds, but when the city grew up around us the need for a cat was gone but the desire for a cat remained. The desire for this strange animal was passed down to me.

I currently am the owner of three cats. Each cat has been affectionately nicknamed "Stupid" and they each love my Commodore machines. I would on cool days find one "stupid" lying on my printer, another "stupid" sleeping on a drive, and a third "stupid" licking her front paws while on the keyboard. If there was anywhere else I would have Commodore equipment stored, running or not, they would think of it as a resting place. "Fat Boy isn't using it, so I will," is what I think is going through their minds at the time.

With this out in the open, think about what it's like to run a bulletin board system with all this cat activity, or non-activity, whatever is best. Anytime I would come home and find a user kicked off, or my keyboard locked in mini-terminal mode all night just because some cat was bedding down, or just passing through and they decided to use the keyboard as an off ramp.

Now let's confuse the factors with a catfight or two (that should be "stooge" fights) that occur while more than one cat staked territorial rights over a Commodore piece while I was using the machine. I am grateful to God that out of all the scuffles no machinery was damaged but I know that because of such activity my repair person charged me extra just for cleaning out the cat hair.

Even as I typed this article into the word processor some "stupid" tried to traverse the keyboard in hopes of making it to an open window close by. She had to stop just long enough for me to acknowledge her existence and pet her white fur, so I picked her up and placed her into the window next to the computer stand. I personally think they stop just to get a breeze from the mini fan I have mounted to my workstation. Right now she has jumped out of the window and chose instead to lay down on the now active 1541. Has she no respect? Has she no shame? Nah!!

"If they're such a nuisance, then get rid of them," some would say. Quite frankly, I can't. They are just a part of my personal culture as my Commodore machines are. I can't ask you to get rid of something you really enjoy, can I? That would be ridiculous on the both of us. I truly keep a cat around to remind me of my dad who also loved cats. Machines can be cleaned, the house dusted and the Commodore locked out from sysop use, but the cats are mainly for a memorial. There's very little the cats do except lie around and get fat anyway, but it sure is odd to be typing on the computer and the next thing that happens is a set of paws steps over your hands and a feline body blocks your view of the monitor. The animal stops to look at you, displaying some sort of expression that could be interpreted as approval, then it moves on. Sometimes it makes me wonder - wonder enough to say, "Thanks, Dad. I'm glad to see that you're still proud of me."

THE NEW FAÇADE TO –
"RAIDERS AT MIDNIGHT"

I watched my cats as they did whatever it is cats do while messing with my Commodore 128 one night and wrote it down in an espionage style story which was very popular among the other Commodore users groups that our club exchanges newsletters with. This story has been reprinted several times back then and people enjoyed the spy type styling of the piece and even sent comments back to our Commodore users group on how much they enjoyed it. It made the Commodore more fun. I remember working on this piece in the basement of my job on one of my many breaks we took. I had pen and paper as well as a dictionary and thesaurus on hand to make sure I used as many different words that I could to make sure redundancy was not a part of the story.

I was excited to write this story down and couldn't wait for it to come to being as it burned in my brain, demanding to be released onto paper. I even had an instructor look the paper over to make sure everything was understandable and the reader could picture everything in their minds as they read. She did have some difficulty with the "silver snakes" that I referred to and I had to explain to her that these were strings that were used to pull my software pouch together. This pouch was an old make up bag of my wife's that she was going to discard after using its contents but I convinced her to let me use it as a 5.25 disk carrying case when I had to take my Commodore to the club meetings. It only carried about six disks but it was handy it making transport of disks easier and more organized.

Please enjoy the next selection. It was fun to write and fun to read as I remember the night these animals made their nightly trek over my Commodore computer stand.

RAIDERS AT MIDNIGHT

The one in yellow goes first. He quickly but stealthily climbs up the nearby gray-colored structure and balances himself on its top. Looking at the expanse between himself and his destination, he, for a moment, ponders the times that he has missed this vault before him and plummeted to the floor below, but he sees no other alternative. He must traverse this expanse to make his intended destination.

He looks back. His white-clad compatriot joins him on the structure and she awaits his next move. Cautiously he takes a few steps backwards to grant himself running room. Then, in starting position, he focuses his attention on his target and at the sounding of an imaginary starting gun he lunges forward quickly, speeding to the edge of the edifice. Upon reaching the edge, with a final burst of energy, he bounds off the structure and finds himself for a moment, airborne.

His mind and eyes are fixed fast upon his landing site knowing perfectly well that there is no backing out at this point, but his vision soon shifts as he notices himself dipping far sooner than his strategically calculated leap was intended. He stretches out, hoping to grab the top ledge of his target as he passes.

Over on the former complex, his white-clad cohort steps to the edge and watches in horror as her yellow-draped friend begins to drop to the floor below. But his fall is short lived as he successfully but painfully makes contact with the top ledge of the edifice across the way. She grimaces as she hears his legs and chest slam against the high wall, but she quickly breathes a sigh of relief as she notes that he, for the most part, is all right. She watches in charged anticipation as he struggles to lift himself onto the top of his landing place.

He pulls his pelted personage onto the framework of wood and screws, and in his newly weakened state, steps sluggishly away from the border. He turns and looks across the way back at his comrade, giving her a confident glance that he is all right and everything is going as planned. "I'm getting too old for this," he thinks to himself.

"He's getting too old for this," she thinks to herself as she begins to prepare to make the same leap. But out of the corner of her eye, illuminated by a glimmer of moonlight, was a route that would take her out of harm's way. She strides to the west to where she sees a narrow balcony-like protrusion coming from a wall; a plank that traverses the chasm. The old timer across the way watches as she walks up to the rail less bridge. Glancing past the walkway, she sees the blackened abyss that almost claimed her partner. Even though this looks safer, she still holds reservations of its stability. Placing one foot carefully on this free standing protrusion, she tests its sturdiness. It's strong. She places another foot on it; soon she is walking balanced and poised across the bridge and effortlessly steps off when she reaches the other side. She joins her yellow-attired ally, who stares in disbelief at her smirk, then shakes his head.

They both turn together to face the object of their affections, the reason why they are taking such risks, the cause of their night assault – the Commodore 128 computer.

They stride towards the keyboard, the face of which is dimly lit by the moon, making an endeavor to shine, despite the trees wrestling to snuff out its luminance. Stepping up, they stride gracefully across this classic ciphering machine, making sure their combined weight does not crush the casing. They pass over without incident, stepping down to browse this new land they have uncovered.

Now the ancient one in yellow glances at something from the corner of his eye; his head snaps to the left, waiting wide-eyed for the moon to reveal to him what he is sure he sees. He stares intently, crouching down in case he is identified, waiting for this lesser light to shine once again. Impatience begins to set in. The element of surprise is on his side. He should be able to take down whatever is lurking in the dark. He digs into the surface, hoping to get a grip on the ground to make a speedy lunge towards this new invader. The trees outside divide at the wind's command to flash a glimmer of moonlight once again and the ancient one leaps.

The younger, white-clad lady is having her own set of troubles. Before her lies a flat square object that is protected by two silver snakes. Even without light she can see that the snakes are possibly in hibernation, so if she wants the contents which are in the plastic bag she will have to strike before the argent serpents awaken. She also poises herself like her mentor, digs in and without waiting for light, vaults into action.

The reptiles don't know what hit them. Upon contact with her foes, the snakes recoil at the pounce. The agile lass then grasps them tightly and rolls on her back and using her legs, kicks her adversaries over the east ledge and into the murky blackness, the plastic bag going with them. She rolls to her feet, hurrying to the ledge to see if they were truly gone, but there is nothing but pitch darkness.

The old timer has himself occupied with more than he bargained for. What started out as a fat, brown creature with small rounded ears and a black bowtie as shown by the moonlight, shed this exterior to reveal a hideous, cold, inflexible monster with a slender tail that runs for what appears to be miles. This camouflaged creature has its elongated appendage wrapped several times around the ancient one's pudgy body and despite all his biting and clawing, he can't convince the creature to let go. In a last act of desperation, the seasoned veteran of these midnight raids rotates to the left in hopes of getting the coiled creature to release him. But the monster is too smart for him and mimics his twists and turns. Tumbling and tumbling they go, across the wooden planks and headlong toward the east edge. The lady sees the danger and springs to help her instructor, but even with youth on her side, she is too slow to assist him and she watches in terror as both he and the leviathan twist a final time, then tumble off the east ledge and plummet into the darkness, still locked in mortal combat. They both fade into obscurity.

Panic and anxiety flow through the veins of this espionage debutante as she contemplates the worst. Her hero, her coach, is gone. But she has to know, could he have survived? Despite his age, he is resilient, especially in a crisis. She decides to find out. Retracing her steps, she hastens back across the Commodore 128, traverses the chasm again via the rail less bridge, and descends the gray structure which led them into this fiasco. In the darkness she stands, waiting for her eyes to adjust as much as possible to the deep murkiness, but the uneasiness in her breast forces her to press on. Feeling around with each step, as rapidly as she can, she begins the search for her elder nurturer. Slowly her eyes adjust to the night, just enough for her to see the final resting place of her senior.

He is sprawled out on his right side, his legs extended forward from his body. The hydra he battled lies motionless underneath him, apparently exterminated by the fall. The white-garbed pupil presupposes that the monster released him upon its demise, but all too late for him. She steps forward to get a closer look at his carcass, checking his face for any signs of life. From what she could tell in the darkness, his gaze is fixed forward, devoid of any signs of life. She hangs her head low in mourning, then turns slowly to leave.

The aged one sits up with a start and shakes his head to clear the cobwebs. The young one spins on her heels at the sound of stirring behind her. Cautiously, she steps up to him in disbelief. She saw him dead, or so she thought. She thought wrong, for there he is, alive but a little shaken. He turns his head to gaze at her with the same look he gave her upon the platform just a few minutes earlier. She brightens, happy that her colleague has survived this ordeal.

Suddenly, a flash of white light cleaves the darkness from the east; so bright this aurora that it brings temporary blindness to both of them. Then from behind this artificial sun comes thunder; an echo that penetrates every fiber of their beings. A resonance that, to the acoustics, appears to be forming words:

"WHAT'S GOING ON IN HERE?"

Both the yellow one and the white one know that they have been caught. The elder leaps to his feet and makes a break for it, darting away from the scene. Following quickly behind him is his associate, scrambling through sector after sector until they reach their hideaway. They duck, lumbering into the aperture and going deeply into the complex in hopes of escaping the booming sound.

"OH, MAN! WHAT A MESS!" says the rumble. "MY SOFTWARE POUCH AND 1351 MOUSE ARE ON THE FLOOR!" it continues. "I'M GONNA KILL YOU CATS FOR THIS!"

The felines lick their paws, ever content in the outcome of the nocturnal accomplishment. They give each other a fleet, satisfying glance then return to their ritualistic cleansing. "Tomorrow," they each think, "is another night."

DA DE LUM DUMB -- DA DE LUM DUM DUMB!

Thor, the ancient feline and Puff his white haired accomplice were found guilty of attempted sabotage of a Commodore 128. They were sentenced to expulsion from their domicile for a night, but allowed to return by the next morning and are reported to be behaving well after this experience.

THE NEW FAÇADE TO-
"A CALL TO LIFE"

It would appear that the façade to this piece will be longer than the piece itself. This paragraph, first presented for an actual grade in college, is the Obadiah of this edition of a Commodore testament, being short and yet full of power as I tried desperately to capture in words the look of a Commodore computer as it sits on the computer stand waiting to be booted. The sad point of this whole piece is that I only got a mediocre grade for it, but after reviewing it for this edition, with my new knowledge of writing and structure, I can see why, but I am leaving this paragraph in its present form so you can read it for yourself.

When it came time for me to try and return to college to broaden my writing career, the new college contacted my old college to try and retrieve my transcripts, but somehow my entire existence of attending the former college was wiped out of their computers. Nothing was left of me at all, as though I never attended. This includes my work done in the writing class, this paragraph included. The only way this piece remained was on a 5.25 disk in my vast Commodore collection of writing, and in the first edition of Run/Stop-Restore.

There is not much to comment on a paragraph other than what has been said before. I do recall how I struggled to keep all I wanted to say about the Commodore down to one paragraph, but I wanted it to sound more like a sleeping entity waiting to be woke up, and I think that I accomplished that pretty well here, even if my instructor couldn't quite see it my way. So please enjoy this short narrative of a Commodore waiting to come to life.

A CALL TO LIFE

The Commodore 128 computer rests quietly on the brown stand that it calls home waiting for the flick of the black toggle switch on the upper right along the base of the machine and bring it to cybernetic life. Its sloped beige casing is smooth and without marks despite its endless years of service to all from destructive toddler to determined adult. The keys on its face are worn and suffer from battle damage through years of combat. Above it, suspended on a thick brown board is a white plastic box containing a light black cathode ray tube, called the monitor. It also awaits anxiously for activation so its screen can glow bright in electric neon blues informing of available bytes and the present basic version currently in memory. To its right, sitting in a row prepared for military inspection, are the four tan rectangular cubes that the Commodore refers to as its disk drives, each lined up in order of its speed, size, capacity, and timing ratio; a well organized troop that also shows their wounds of war. At its outermost is the square beige printer standing alone as the final island port of information when all other avenues of digital transportation have come to their prescribed ends. For now the 128 CPU sits, waiting, but no more. The black toggle is pressed; the monitor glows; the drives in red and green lights snap to attention; the printer grinds its spherical print head to a starting point; and the glorious, electrical, silent opera begins.

THE NEW FAÇADE TO –
"A VIEW ON GEOS"

Since I last published this article I have learned a great deal on how to get around the Commodore operating system known as GEOS, but I still restrict myself to activities that only have to do with word processing. Since the last edition I now work on two newsletters for Commodore clubs; one is printed monthly and the other every two months, but both newsletters are written using the GEOS word processing program called GEOWrite. Along with this achievement I have also written, submitted, and actually got published, several articles using GEOWrite, avoiding the use of a Microsoft based word processing package completely. Many printers that cooperate with the Commodore and GEOWrite can access the near letter quality (NLQ) function of the program and make the text look just as professional as clean as though it was printed using a modern printer and an IBM based word processing package. I have always admired the fact that as old as the Commodore is, it can still keep up with the modern machines, especially in some computing circles.

As I stated in this article, our club president brought in a GEOS operating system to demonstrate for us and I thought that it was just another attempt for Commodore to act like an IBM, until I discovered by getting into the program myself that GEOS is the precursor to what Windows is doing now. GEOS was even released for older IBM computers that ran on the MS-DOS systems after it found its success in the Commodore world.

I never got to attend any of the president's special interest seminars on GEOS, as I was hoping to do when I wrote the piece, but what little he taught me over the phone and at club meetings helped me to get enough going to make a strong use of the program. The entire text of Run/Stop-Restore was written and published in GEOWrite, which is a big accomplishment for such a computer with supposedly limited capabilities.

A VIEW ON GEOS

Everybody by now has heard our club president speak and write time and time again about GEOS, the windows-like program for both the Commodore 64 and Commodore 128 computers. He's spoken about how handy and versatile a program GEOS is. I would like add my own two bits about GEOS.

I've been using GEOS 128 v2.0 for only a few months now and I must admit to everyone that this program is phenomenal!! I just have the basic package which includes GEOWrite 2.1, GEOPaint, GEODictionary, GEOSpell, GEOMerge, Text Grabber, -- oh geez, it seems like the variety of material goes on forever. I've only been using GEOWrite and GEOPaint so far. I was apprehensive at first to use GEOS so it sat on my shelf for about two years (I acquired my copy from a BBS buyout at around that time). I didn't have a mouse either so that also held me up, but once I got one there were no longer any excuses. In fact, that excuse was lame since GEOS works with joystick also. I booted GEOS 128 up, which I found to be rather fast, even on a 1541; then I was off -- to the user's manual. I read as much data as I could before I started messing around, but even with all the text at hand, I still had problems. Our president came to my rescue.

While I was working in GEOWrite, I would have to insert a disk containing Desktop 128 after I would CLOSE a file. I posted a message in the CBM-GEOS echo of the Commodore BBS telling of my dilemma and President Rich called me on the phone straightway. He educated me on what I had to do to keep that from happening. He told me to put a copy of Desktop 128 on all of my work disks (a work disk is a disk you format through GEOS to save your personal work, like writings or artwork) and I'll always enter into my working menu without the use of the master disk that contained the original copy of Desktop 128.

GEOS is also a great tutorial for the children. Since school computers are going IBM and IBM is going Microsoft Windows, then GEOS will fit right into this genre quite nicely. With slight variations, any child working on GEOS at home should gain an acquisition to using Windows at school. I personally have found both my sons more adept in the last quarter of the '98-'99 school session than the first quarter because of their using GEOS at home. My six year old loves working on GEOPaint, with all the designs he can call up as well as what he can draw on his own. He's so proud of his creations that he has GEOPaint artwork magnetically adhered to the refrigerator on display for all visitors to his "gallery" to admire. My oldest son likes the idea of having a Windows-like program to work from so he can practice better control of Windows at school (he also is a GEOPaint nut!).

So what do I do with GEOS? As a novice to this program I must confess that I don't do much, but I am looking forward to doing plenty more as I get more GEOS programs. I am also looking forward to attending one of the president's GEOS Special Interest Group meetings and learn how to maximize this program to its fullest potential. My latest plans are that I am going to convert some of my Speedscript and Brainpower 128 writing files to GEOWrite files. Right now I do all my writing on GEOWrite for the simple reason that GEOWrite offers more printing, fonts, and formatting options than any word processor I own.

I would like to encourage anyone who hasn't tried GEOS with their Commodore to at least test it out. I know that GEOS isn't for everyone, but at the same time there might be something that GEOS has that you as a Commodore user might need or have been looking for and cannot find it as a stand-alone program. GEOS isn't harmful to your health and does not produce CFC's that can damage the ozone layer. I'm hoping to collect and use all the GEOS programs that I find that will assist me in my personal as well as business endeavors. I know, for example, that President Rich has shown a video demo on GEOS games that includes a solitaire program. I'm putting that on my gift list for the wife. She loves solitaire -- sometimes more than she loves me....

THE NEW FAÇADE TO –
"COMMODORE AND Y2K"

Now this piece is dated. I wondered if I should have included this in the second edition, but in my opinion it gave pertinent information about the work being done to make Commodore programs ready for the year 2000 bug. One of the great things about running this ancient piece of hardware was that the unit itself did not suffer such a problem since it started counting time from the moment of initial boot up and only kept track of how long the computer has been on. It was also a programmable string that many programmers before have accessed and made into a personal clock for the measuring of time so one would not have to search for a separate clock. Some programs like GEOS in particular needed the time set on it because for each access to a GEOS file or program, the computer would stamp the time of saving the data into the program itself, which was handy when you or someone else accessing your work, would like to know when was the last time you accessed or made changes to the work in question.

This article remains in the text of the book as a simple reminder of what we all went through when PCs were on their way of crashing because they didn't understand that 00 is greater than 99. I also wondered if those who invented and reinvented computers ever thought that the device would make it strong into the 21st century like it did, or did they think that this computer fad would die out before the year 2000 and something better would take its place. I suppose that information is lost in the chips and resistors of machines gone by.

COMMODORE AND Y2K

I don't know about you, but I've been hearing about the Y2K problem since October of 1998. I guess I'm a little slow. After all, I am from Kansas. But with all that aside, I'm amazed how people who are in the computer business or other careers requiring computer access that depend on the computer are either spending thousands of dollars on people to fix the problem or millions of dollars on replacing the entire system. Personally, I've watched the facility I work at replace every computer in the building at least three times since October 1998. They went from Wyse to Gateway 2000's and now Dells. The big Dells with 19" monitors (who needs a 19" monitor on their desk? It's like everyone watching a Windows 98 demo at each station on TV. Sheesh!)

I don't know the total bill for all this but I pity the folk in my county who have to pay for this in higher taxes. I did talk with the facilities maintenance guys and they were kind enough to tell me that for their department alone it is going to cost approximately $2,200 to upgrade and Y2K proof the program alone that controls the environmental system at our workplace. This price does not include the new Y2K compliant computer system to run the new HVAC program on. If this price is average, then add up the cost of every supervisor, at every facility in county government, throughout my county that is being made Y2K compliant. Now add the cost of a county upgrade to a city government going through the same transition phase. Now multiply that figure by just the 105 counties in Kansas. I don't think there's a calculator made with a digit window that long. Now, just for fun, figure that total for the entire 50 states in this Union, and add the systems needed to run things on a national level. Now, to really nuke your mind, this digit that runs to infinity does not include the private industries that must be Y2K ready by December of this year.

Oh phooey! You've heard all this poo poo before from the experts ranging from the Clinton administration to Microsoft. It's just so frustrating to see all these people lining the pockets of the big wig computer manufacturers at an alarming rate. In the meantime all these non Y2K compliant machines find themselves lining warehouse overstock rooms, at thrift stores, or even in the trash. Where I work we have them scattered sparsely throughout the basement storage facility and in a pile about six feet high and six units across next to the shredder.

All this panic over Y2K and all anyone really would have to do is buy a Commodore computer. Sure, it doesn't have 586K of memory, but it also doesn't have a Y2K complex built into it. Someone at Commodore way back when must have foreseen this problem and made the internal clock (TI$) measure only that time from initial start up, and not keep a constant running clock like most IBMs do.

But before I let my bragging get away with me, I would like to submit for your approval a list of programs that run on Commodore that may have a potential Y2K problem. Please note that as of this writing this list is still expanding and shrinking as more information comes in to approve or disapprove the claims on existing Commodore programs:

GEOS 128: It was brought to my attention through FIDOnet that there might be a patch out there that will fix any Y2K problems this program may have.

GEOCalc: No data in respects to a patch or Y2K upgrade.

GEOPublish: No data in respects to a patch or Y2K upgrade.

GEOCalendar: Word on the FIDOnet suggests that "Commodore World" magazine published a patch to Y2K ready this program some time ago.

GEOWrite: The FIDOnet users also expressed to me that a patch exists for this program as well.

MultiPlan: No data at this time as to a possible Y2K patch

Data Manager: No data at this time as to a possible Y2K patch.

SuperBase: No data at this time as to a possible Y2K patch.

Unzip program CSX01: This program uses a Julian dating method to keep track of files, but Commodore users on the FIDOnet assure me that few if any actually access the date to use this program so more than likely a Y2K patch will not be created for it.

CS DOS: Same problem that exists for the CSX01 and probably will have the same solution as well.

ARC: (including ARC, CSXARC, LHA et. al.) These programs should not have a date problem until the year 2107.

So far this is all that I have gathered over the three months; ten programs out of how many thousands of Commodore programs in existence? What's the percentage ratio on that? Is it better than IBM? Even without a scientific calculator I can tell you YES IT IS!! Now that's pretty impressive in my book. Yet there go all the non-compliant IBMs out the door just to spend thousands on new ones when Commodores are so affordable. For approximately $200 you can get a great set up consisting of a Commodore 128, a 1571 disk drive, a 40/80 column monitor and a printer. My last check on computer prices for non-Y2K compliant IBM 286's, 3.5" hard disk drive with 2.2 megs. of storage space and a green screen monitor is $20 at the local thrift shop. It's a shame, really; a Commodore worth more than an IBM just because of a machine's failure to meet the year 2000 problem. I'm just thankful that I was led to a Commodore before any of this stuff came about. I would have to put my family in hock for $4000 on a system I would have to trash by December 31, 1999 and buy all new equipment. It's sad.....real sad.....

I would like to thank all the people both in the Commodore User Group as well as those Commodore users around the world, from Australia to Israel and points beyond, for their help in researching this article. During the collection and editing of information given to me I'm sure that somewhere there might be a misinterpretation of facts. If you know of such a misrepresentation then please inform me.

TENTH ANNIVERSARY UPDATE: Now that this entire stink over Y2K is behind us, I should mention that I myself had to write up a new program patch for the Money Manager type in program from RUN magazine. This program refused to allow the user to make progressive changes month to month because it didn't recognize the year 2000 and beyond. I managed to fix that problem with a few lines of code and the program works fine now. If anyone is still using the program let me know and I will send you the updated program.

THE NEW FAÇADE TO--
"I'M AN IDIOT"

I am glad to have this chance to write this article since it follows the path of the fight with CDC. As explained in the article, I grew up a little and learned that all is not lost. The club was ready to front the money to help in my cause to lease Check It Out from CDC, but I refused the offer and went on ahead to write the companion and upgrade Check It Out. I also talk quite a bit about the work done on Obligator Coordinator 1.5, which I have converted and developed into The Ledger, which is also talked about elsewhere in this book.

Obligator Coordinator versions 1.0 (copyrighted) and 1.5 both allow the user to keep track of the bills that are paid in your house or business and save all the changes onto disk whenever the user presses the SAVE key. I have not worked on this program in years and I thought it lost, but back then I really was getting to get some use of it. I remember taking this program to the club and trying to get everyone to sign a beta test agreement. One person at the club, a newbie, was ready to sign but found a discrepancy in the contract and debated with me for about a half an hour on the wording on the agreement. All I wanted to do was protect my work and make sure none of these people stole what I was doing. I don't remember is she ever took a copy or signed an agreement, but I do remember people giving it a good once over and showing me both the strengths and weakness of same.

As you can tell by the next article, I have fun writing programs, books, articles, and documentations. I just pray that you have just as much fun with your hobby as I do with mine.

I'M AN IDIOT!

Did you ever get so frustrated that you have to stop whatever it was you were doing, leave said situation, and come back to it later? I've been practicing this little piece of advice from my doctor for quite a while now and found it quite relaxing; so much so that I've applied it to other factors of my life, including my work with the Commodore. But before I go much further I need to apologize to everyone who reads this article and those who have been following my scribbling all this time. I have done a lot of useless whining about this person or that program over the last twelve to eighteen months. By stepping back and observing my situation from afar, I've been able to see things from a new perspective. Let's start with a look at my ongoing situation with Ceramic Dynamic Computers.

CDC is the owner of my program "Check It Out!" There's nothing I can do about it; that's the way the contract I signed reads; so I have to stop my useless whining and deal with it from that point. After a long conversation with our club president, I have been brought a different approach on how I can get what I need from CDC, and that approach is called "licensing." I've always known about licensing a program but my research was mainly from the license owner's point-of-view and not the person who is requesting the license. By the time this article makes the newsletter I will have contacted CDC and negotiations will be on the way to get a licensing agreement signed and progress done on some programs I am sitting on.

Another thing I've been a fool on is my hurrying the work on "Obligator Coordinator 1.0." I wanted to have this program done by summer of 1998, but it wasn't until Christmas of that same year that I presented the work for beta testing. All those who participated in the test gave me new insights into it, so I made adjustments, and ran into some problems with those adjustments; problems so mean that I put the program away for a good nine months while I did something else. Now I've pulled it out, worked on it some more, and made all the corrections I can with a new perspective, and even if I do say so myself, the changes are marvelous. The program seems to flow smoothly and gives you, the user, easier access to all your functions, plus it helps if I have a properly functioning Commodore 64 to type the code in.

My upgrade, called "Obligator Coordinator 1.5," or "OC v1.5" for short, gives everyone hopefully what they asked for. First up was an error trap on a "DEVICE NOT PRESENT" message when the user attempts to access the printer. Thanks to Mr. Walker, I have a small subroutine that accesses a quick message telling the user of the problem without crashing the program altogether.

Next up was a directory reader. When I asked the members of the Commodore Users Group for such a reader I got a flood of responses. Many of those that came to me were directory designers and only two were readers: one I found and one that came from Mr. Walker. Naturally my ego told me to merge my reader with "OC v1.5" and put Mr. Walker's on a disk and shelve it. Now my ego was going to pay me back.

At every filename request, the user could type "DIR" and the directory would be read to the screen, but with my directory reader after the reading the program locked up. I wrestled with this for months not allowing humility to set in and believing that my directory reader could be the problem. Finally out of frustration I put "OC v1.5" away. Now, nine months later, with that fresh view I mentioned earlier, I have ceded to my humility and found that Mr. Walker's reader was more Commodore friendly, so I scrapped my directory reader and permanently inserted his.

While running "Obligator Coordinator 1.0," I stumbled across an error that missed even the beta testing. When the user was building his debt file, he couldn't read the error message when he overtyped the limit set by the program, so I added a carriage return (CHR$(13)) at the end of the error message. Now the message remains on the screen until RETURN is pressed instead of flashing across the screen in a fleet second.

Finally, I reduced the number of spaces in the CR$ (creditor string input) and N$ (notation string input) from seventy to thirty characters, not knowing at the time I was dealing with a bad memory chip inside my Commodore 64 as well as the aforementioned lock up with the directory reader. I though the problem lied in my N$ and CR$ inputs, so at that time I reduced them from seventy to sixty. When the program still refused to function, I again did a reduction from sixty to fifty, then from fifty to forty, finally stopping at thirty. After a nine month hiatus from programming and some earlier corrections, the input statements work fine. The reason the CR$ and N$ strings stay at thirty characters is to make the file easier to read when used in viewing mode. The whole package makes a nice block on the screen, full of color and information.

The biggest change came from the boot programs. "Obligator Coordinator 1.0" had boot programs, but for some reason the boot did not load the main program. It was so bad that after forty lines of text was loaded into memory, the program collapsed, so I took the boots out of the first version. The Commodore Man gave me a copy of "Compute Gazette" from December 1985 and in this magazine was an article on program chaining. I followed the instructions listed and now my boot programs work with "OC v1.5" perfectly. When the user types LOAD"*",8,1 in 64 mode, he will get a graphic greeting, followed closely by a second screen which contain the loading command menu where the user can go on to "OC v1.5" or exit to BASIC. As more programs are developed, I hope to chain them to the loader and make them part of the debt management series package.

For GEOS nuts, I have transferred all of "OC v1.5" programs and boots onto a GEOS formatted disk so GEOS users should be able to load "OC v1.5" as a GEOS file and click onto the C64 file marked "OC v1.5" and avoid the loaders altogether. Due to the disk open/close commands written in BASIC 2.0 and not 7.0, "OC v1.5" will only work in 64 mode. For the next upgrade I'll probably try to make "Obligator Coordinator" work in both 64 and 128 modes as well as 40/80 column screens. Sorry, I didn't change the icon for the GEOS load since I don't know how this is done. Maybe someone will be nice enough to show me how to do this. I'm also looking at modulating many of the larger subroutines so editing the program to fit your personal criteria will be easier.

I do hope that the changes, corrections, and improvements to "Obligator Coordinator" meet everyone's approval. Those of you who are currently using "Obligator Coordinator 1.0" please let me know so I can get you the upgrade; but before any of that is done, I would like to make another beta test run with "OC v1.5" to see if anyone else can find faults with its makeup. I would especially appreciate any suggestions on how to make the screens easier on the eye. Right now I have a black background, and for the on screen text I use the other fifteen colors.

I am personally impressed with "Obligator Coordinator Version 1.5" and I hope you can share in my enthusiasm as you use and apply this debt manager to your everyday business life.

THE NEW FAÇADE TO—
"SO MUCH TO DO, SO LITTLE TIME"

When one gets a chance to sit down in a quiet state of mind and evaluate what one needs to do, a list starts to form that can actually start to get so big that it can begin to destroy the mind. Only when a person starts to pick and choose his method of operation carefully can one find himself slowly and painstakingly working from beginning the final end of a list of projects.

This next entry shows how I used the printed word of our little newspaper to create a list of chores that needed to be done on the Commodore, how I was hoping to execute each one, and bring them finally to some sort of accomplishment. One of the big reasons I did this from time to time is to let users know exactly what it was I was working on or planning to work on and I would hope on getting some kind of early feedback on it in hopes of getting some kind of direction, but then again, they had no idea what I was working on any more than I did. My readers were smart for me to finish the program work and present it before they started the criticisms.

I pray that as you read this and understand what I was trying to accomplish, that you will think of your own circle of confidants that would be kind enough to be brutally honest when you started working on something. It has been said in ancient texts that there is good counsel in the group of numbers, especially those who only look out for what is best for you, and conversely, they look for the same thing from you so when it becomes your turn be as candid but as loving as they have been to you, or sometimes, maybe even a little more kinder.

SO MUCH TO DO, SO LITTLE TIME

I've been going through some of the Commodore stuff I want to revamp, and it seems like the list goes on for a short distance. Please remember, while I am trying to re-do some Commodore work I am also working on other writing projects, too; but more on that some other time. The three programs that I am looking at for the moment is: Check It Out, Check File Creator, and TEA 4 2. I'll try to go through what I have seen and what I want to do one at a time, starting with Check It Out.

Even though the original Check It Out was good enough to get into the pages of RUN magazine, with what I have learned about Commodore programming of recent, it seems that it's possible to make this program work better than what it did in RUN. Besides, one of reason why Check It Out looked the way it did in the magazine was the agreements in the work for hire contract I signed. The program can be no more than twenty six blocks long. Even with all the crunching I did to get it to twenty six blocks, the program was still a rough draw, and on top of that, I didn't know at the time the program was only going to work best with the Commodore MPS 802 printer, which is the printer I worked with for the year it took me to write the program. I have been trying to find a replacement MPS 802 printer to begin my work again, but so far there has been no luck in getting it. So the first order of business is to find a printer that works as well as or better than the MPS 802. I am thinking that the Star NX10-C might be a good performer in this endeavor, and I think I can get a hold of one from one of the Commodore clubs out east.

The next step is to start making the program flow a lot better. When I started crunching the program, I should have moved all the crunched lines of data scattered throughout the work and placed them at the beginning of the program as part of the set up. I also need to divide the program into its subroutines and label them accordingly. I would also like to make it to where, like TEA and TEA 4 2, you can view the check before it is printed on. I know that there is already a preview section to the check, but I don't know if it sufficient or not. At the time it was, but now, well, I may let beta testing tell me if an update of the preview is needed or not.

One thing I would like to do is allow the account numbers that are sometimes necessary on a check that goes to a corporation requiring one is to move that data down to the memo section of the check, but since the printer I used had a habit of syntaxing before that part of the check could be printed on, I may have to leave the account number where it is – at the top of the check. Other than that, there's nothing else I can think of to do with Check It Out.

On to Check File Creator - Holy crap! I never knew that this program was hurting so bad, and I thought it was ready for the unveiling in the next issue of RUN. Maybe it was a good thing that RUN ended its publication after Check It Out was published, otherwise there would be another bad program somehow finding it's way among the good programs that RUN was so famous for. First of all, I need to change the name of the work from Check File Creator to CheckMate. This makes it sound much cooler. I will be referring to the latter name for the rest of this article. I also noticed that when the computer went to access the disk drive for writing to the disk, the operation light came on and stayed on. Not a good thing, especially if something happens to the computer like a power failure, then the disk drive would create a splat file and the disk would have to be validated before any more work could be done. I will have to re-write the entire sequential file subroutine to collect data first; then write the information to the disk.

Another thing is compatibility with Check It Out. It would seem that running together each program by making a LOAD command in each of them is not going to work out as well as first thought. Remember, both CheckMate and Check It Out must cooperate together as one working program, even though they are two, in order to make the project a success. Ken Clayton a long time ago gave me some POKE and PEEK commands that allows programs to cooperate together in order to make them work as one but that is for loading a series of programs as one, but not to swap back and forth between programs. Even though I have them for TEA 4 2, getting the POKE commands to work interchangeably might prove to be difficult. This is where help from the Commodore community at large will come in handy. I will need a command line or a subroutine that will allow the users of both Check It Out and CheckMate to use the programs interchangeably without the programs "crashing" into each other, as it were, while one is being overwritten by the other, and vice versa.

Next for CheckMate is making it more like its cousin Check It Out. Both programs will have a similar set up, but when CheckMate is used to write a check, this will eliminate the use of half of the functions of Check It Out. Check It Out will them be capable of printing the check off quickly. Check It Out will still be able to write checks, if the user still wishes to use the functions in the program. The reason for CheckMate is so that the user of Check It Out won't have to input repetitive checks that need to be paid every month for the same amount. CheckMate creates a permanent check in a sequential file that is easily called up using an upgraded Check It Out. It sounds kind of simple, doesn't it? Also, the thought of adding opening graphics to each program, like I did TEA 4 2, has crossed my mind, but with the programs designed to overwrite each other, such graphics might be a bit over dramatic. I have to remember the K.I.S.S. system – Keep It Simple, Stupid – but as simple as the program can be, it is still going to require a lot of work to get the program ready for basic Commodore use.

Finally for TEA 4 2 – this program is pretty much where I want it to be thanks to all the wonderful hands in the Commodore community with their beta testing help. I do want to make the program to work in Commodore 128 mode, and I was thinking of making it work in 80 column, but laziness sets in when I run TEA 4 2 in 128 mode since it looks so well in 40 column. The color is a little off, but for the most part the program still works in this mode. This upgrade for TEA 4 2, which will be called TEA PAR T, or whatever else comes up that sounds better, will be the last upgrade for the program. Unless there comes up a need to make the program better past TEA PAR T, then it shall end here. The one thing I see that is needed to make the program better is a subroutine that will allow another selection from the print menu. I see that some envelopes have only one window instead of two, like the kind of envelope TEA 4 2 was written for. The next upgrade will allow the choice of someone to print onto a sheet of paper for only the one window envelope. Like I said in previous articles that I have addressed this idea, TEA 4 2 already works like this, but the paper prints a loose comma in the From Address area of the form. This is a carry-over from TEA 4 2, but it still works. The Single Window subroutine will eliminate the comma and just scroll down through the page and start printing the To Address subroutine. Also, the single window envelope has that window inset about three to five spaces more to the right than it does in double window envelopes. I may just add to the print subroutine the necessary extra spaces to make the envelope look more professional and neat.

One thing is for sure that all the programs are going to need their respective documentations re-written. Check It Out and CheckMate do not have on screen documentation since they were suppose to go to RUN magazine, so a start from scratch is going to be necessary. TEA PAR T has most of its documentation done from the previous versions, but a quick explanation of the new subroutine should be included. I also was thinking about adding the auto-boot subroutine to the 128 version. Lord Ronin of ACUG said that the 128 demo disk has the auto-boot on it that can be added to any created program. I will look into this.

Now the big question: When will all these projects get their time on the Roach Hotel Commodore keyboard? I have it on the template to get the all done sometime before the 2011 Commodore expositions season begins anew, which I think the first big one is on Memorial Day. I tried to go to this one in 2009, but money prevented us from attending. Now here's the deal on this revised plan – I hope to have three programs and the new edition of Run/Stop – Restore to take with me to the conventions for sale or trade. I will talk more about the revamp being planned for Run/Stop-Restore in another issue of the newsletter.

Thank you for allowing me to use the pages of our magazine to plan out the itinerary for the upcoming work being scheduled for the Roach Hotel. Please keep your reading eye here in this magazine for further developments in anything Commodore coming from us.

THE NEW FAÇADE TO - "BIRTH OF A COMMODORE INNOVATION"

This is an article I wrote about a Commodore work in progress called The Ledger. I first had the program copyrighted as The Obligator Coordinator, but with the advancement of time and the growth of my Commodore knowledge, The Obligator Coordinator became obsolete. Sadly, also, the program in its first form was hard to work with. The new version is much easier to run and very easy to understand in the way it presented the information to the user.

For anyone who has owned or ran any of my previous programs, they will note that The Ledger works basically on the same principle as those, with menus, submenus, and sequential files being accessed and manipulated except for each one the function of the program is different. I get to present this work and others like it at Commodore conventions all over the United States and I even get to demonstrate them on some occasions. I have fun doing this for the reason being that I get to use a little of my stage training from my high school days mixed in with a little of the comedy training I had during my short stint in stand up back in the 1980s.

This piece is my progress with the work and what I had done with it to that date. Sometimes getting something written, whether it is in a program or a book, just takes the initiative to sit down and do it. Don't worry about mistakes for they can always be found a corrected. Just as long as things come out the way you want it in the final draft is all that matters. I hope I can relay to you, the reader, how much fun and frustration it was to make this little program. Please enjoy.

BIRTH OF A COMMODORE INNOVATION

Once again the geniuses at the Roach Hotel's science and technology center have come up with a really, really great product especially made for the Commodore 64 on the Commodore 128, and what is this new innovation? Why it is no more than the latest from the Roach Hotel – The Ledger! The Ledger is a BASIC program that allows the user to have ready access to information needed on any bill, so if quick access is required, all that is needed to be done is to LOAD and RUN the program, then call off the name of the bill, and the information is right there and ready to be read off! Groovy!

I know I have talked about creating The Ledger for a few issues now and thanks to a little inspiration and some doctor's orders ("Go do something relaxing to take your mind off your worries"), I sat down one night after work at the Commodore 128 and started typing in the code to what has become one of the easiest programs I have written so far (thank God!). The Ledger started out by just working on what I call the "heart," or the main function, of the program. This was the way the program would take the data inputted and calculate it down to the next number, then it will save these new numbers as either the present file, or you can make a new file, keeping the old file as an archive on disk.

In The Ledger, you will be able to view the name of the account, the account number, the web address (if one is available), the address, city state, and zip code of the account, the phone number, and the total amount owed, your minimum payment, and when it is due. One of the suggestions given to me was to add a "Last Pymt On" line in the INPUT statement, but the INPUT right now is maxed out, so it was suggested that I try linking two INPUT lines together using the "semicolon – colon" end command that is used when you want to make a continuing PRINT statement past the eighty character limit. This is the method I use to create my .DOX files when I am writing text for on screen reading. It is a tedious method of writing but it pays off with a great looking on-screen display.

As you might have guessed by now, I took The Ledger files, called "T13," which stands for the thirteenth test program, to the March meeting and ran the disk for them to look at and criticize. Scott and Jack, the only two attendees outside myself, came up with several great ideas that would improve the program.

1. Change the "Amt. Due" to "Min Pymt. Due" – This was confusing to Scott and Jack when I show an "Amt. Owed" and an "Amt. Due" section. Don't they mean the same thing? Basically not, since one is what is owed and the other is what the company to whom money is owed will accept for that receipt, but it was a good idea so I incorporated it into the program.

2. Change the "Save Data As" command to an "Archive This Data" command – I thought this was a good idea since what you will be basically doing is creating the file and archiving the data onto disk for future payment reference and billing information.

3. Show "Min. Pymt. Due" and ask if you want to pay that amount – This is what I was doing, or so I thought, with the "Amt. Due" input command, but this feature allows the user to select the "Min. Pymt. Due" display and use that stored information to pay on screen and subtract that from the "Amt. Owed" display.

4. Make a new Pymt. Amt. – I have done this and it will be in section four of the program where the user updates his file when a new bill from an existing account (like the electric or gas bill) comes in the mail. This function will allow the user to update the "Amt. Owed," "Min Pymt. Due," and the "When?" input sections.

5. Update the "Amt. Owed" – This function can now be done at either section three or section four of the program. Section three makes the actual payment, which updates the file before saving. Section four is the update when a new bill comes in, as I have stated previously.

6. Don't give an option to update the "Amt. Due" – In my haste to program The Ledger, I made Section Three and Section Four to basically do the same thing. Section Four is just a recalibration of data as it renews while Section Three makes the actual payment. Section Three grants you the option. Now it does not. It will show you what was done to the file data before you select the "Archive Data" command. If you don't like it, then press N and the program goes back to the home screen.

7. A "Paid On" input - As stated previously, I am going to work on creating a longer INPUT string for this command, otherwise, I think I can squeeze one more command onto the original INPUT string. I will have to re-string the present data, but it shouldn't be too hard, Lord willing.

8. Look into making all the INPUT read off of one SEQ file - right now the program is set for the user to create his own data file for each bill inputted into the computer and the user will have to call off each bill and manipulate the data and type in either a new FILENAME or choosing the given option to overwrite the present data with the new data. A continuous read would make for more data to be saved onto one disk, and it is possible, except that I don't understand the concept, even when I read the instructions in the user's guides. I even have programs that do this, but I can't seem to lift the code off of the program and make it work for me. I will investigate this further and see what I can come up with.

When done I hope to make The Ledger a major arsenal in the combat against debt and the need for paper filing systems by creating a computer based filing system that a person can access and make it work for you.

I want to thank Jack and Scott for coming to the March meeting and giving me all this great input. Scott, in his own venerable way, was kind enough to point out a spelling error I made when typing in a PRINT command line, so that was instantly corrected and the program was updated using the SAVE WITH REPLACE (@) command. Smooth. I hope when I bring the changes back to the club in April, I will have some things to show attendees concerning the updates. I would like to have The Ledger up and ready for beta testing sometime by this summer. I still have some more programs to work on, all of this to get ready to go on Commodore book tour sometime next year.

THE NEW FAÇADE TO –
"MY FIGHT WITH CDC"

The story you are about to read is true. Names have been changed to protect the innocent. It wasn't until I became an owner of a copyright that I started to see what CDC was talking about. You just don't go throwing around these important pieces of government paperwork like they are Frisbees. You really have to sit on them and make sure that no one takes what you have worked on so hard to get. But when I wrote Check It Out I was so excited that I just signed away everything I had to do with it just so I can say to world, "I'm a published writer!" Mrs. Roach and I celebrated so much after we got that miniscule royalty check that we just took the family to pizza. At this time RUN had shut its doors and CDC owned the RUN program archive and I was just trying to get the companion program to Check It Out released and out into the Commodore community, but they had the rights and I had squat because I sold my rights for a bowl of red stew.

Now it is ten years later. As of this writing I have unearthed both Check It Out and the companion program, looked them over, and said, "This crud was worth something?" With age does come maturity, I suppose. I have advanced as a writer of notes and a programmer of Commodore and I still find both things fun to do. It seems like nothing is better than to write a couple of subroutines and them run them and watch them work on first attempt; conversely, it is equally as frustrating to do the same motion and watch the code disintegrate into a pile of SYNTAX ERROR messages. But like a fine wine, with a little patience and careful working, what you end up with is something so glorious that you about write a sonnet giving God the glory for the great victory you have won on the final day when all works just like it should.

MY FIGHT WITH CDC

Whenever you ask your neighbor to borrow a hammer, usually the answer is, "Sure, just as long as I get it back." Whenever I seem to ask Ceramic Dynamic Computers to borrow, license, or even pay for programming rights, the answer is usually, "Send us a letter describing what you are planning to do with the program in question and we'll get back to you." I have sent "said information" in a letter three times now and so far I got nothing back. Whoops! Let me take some of that back - I did receive something back once. A little notation scribbled into my original note I mailed to them stating that the copyright notice is essential. I don't quite understand what "essential" means in this case. Does it mean that they wish to still have controlling rights even over my additions to the "Check It Out" program, or do they wish just acknowledgement that the original text is copyright 1992 by CDC with additional material copyright 19xx by Lenard Roach? I have yet to get a straight answer on this.

Dear readers of this column, it has been my nightmare dealing with Ceramic Dynamic Computers about the matter of adding text changes to the original "Check It Out" program I wrote in 1992 for the then RUN magazine. What I wish to do is make a menu driven listing in the middle of the text every time I add a program that pertains to the subject of financial management. For the record, I have one program written, one in re-write and a third in the development stages. I would prefer to make each program available to Commodore users as they are completed instead of waiting until all packages are done and release them as a conglomerate set.

I sometimes ask the question: Is CDC being a complete jerk about this matter? I mean, the program is just sitting there not gaining any profit (I am supposing here), why should they be so hard-nosed? After reading such novels as "Legal Care for Your Software" by Daniel Remer and "How to Copyright Software" by a Mr. Salome, I can understand some of what

CDC is trying to protect. To surrender some of its rights to a program means they are opening a Pandora's Box to anything that could legally slip in. Without proper wording on the documentation granting the permission for me to rework "Check It Out," I could rightly steal the object code and do something totally different with it altogether.

From my understanding of the law, a written work has to be at least eighty percent original before it can be considered a stand-alone work worthy of its own copyright. Anything less of that is considered a derivative work and not copyrightable by the adaptor and any violations to that effect is subject to criminal prosecution. My changes to "Check It Out" will probably be about fifteen to twenty percent original, so there should be no fear from CDC for me to make an original copy at this point, but then this is where my interest would to come into play.

The menu driven boot will call upon other programs that are at best ninety percent original work. I can claim that these new works are original works of "Check It Out" but they do use some of the object code from the same. I can either (A), re-write the object code to where it is one hundred percent free of "Check It Out's" object code or (B), prove in a court of law that the new programs are ninety percent non-reliant and therefore original works and deserving of their own copyright.

"Okay," you may say, "create the works one hundred percent compliant of free standing code and save yourself this fight." Fair enough. I've done that with one written ("Obligator Coordinator v1.0"), and with the other in progress ("Pay Schedule v1.0"), but "Check File Creator," a speedier adaption of "Check It Out," cannot be done that way. I've made it about sixty percent original and that's the best I can do. I also want the boot menu to be able to access "Check It Out" and "Check File Creator" to make the whole thing one big, happy family of programs.

Before he passed away in November of 1998, my best friend and "father" in the Commodore computer, Carl Zuel, suggested that I totally recreate a new "Check It Out" with a directory scan, changeable fonts, etc. That would have been a great idea but I, for one, am not that talented of a programmer and, for two, the recreated work would still be considered a derivative of the original "Check It Out." To clarify a derivative versus original program, let's say, another person unknowing writes a similar program just like "Check It Out" and copyrights it. He goes to a software publisher and gets it published and marketed. I stumble across his program one day while shopping in my favorite software store and see his work. I get a hold of the software publisher (for this argument let's use the programmer as the publisher) and decide to sue him for copyright infringement. We have our day in court. The judge would have to look at both copies of the object code and if he determines that each work is not a derivative of the other, then the new work is free to continue to be sold with its present copyright intact. However, if both programs are named the same, the other person might want to check into changing the name. This is how we get so many different kinds of word processing programs and different style of games using the same format.

So what's to become of me and my continued battle with Ceramic Dynamic Computers? I'm not sure. Both correspondence and phone conversations have been to the negative the last two rounds. I pray I still have a few options left up my sleeve, but from what I know of the law, I don't have many more right off. My advising attorney says that specialty lawyers like those who deal with copyrights are expensive, but they do get the job done. I can just see myself now dumping six months of my salary into a lawyer's pocket just to publish a string of programs. I think CDC knows this and therefore are being the way they are. Like I said earlier, I think I can see it from their point of view, and as a writer and programmer, I can appreciate that. I just hope they can be a little more lenient with me in this matter. After all, where is this program going anyway?

THE NEW FAÇADE TO-
"COMMODORE GAMES FOR GIRLS"

I do a lot more analysis of my work on the Commodore now ever since I found out that users of the machine actually take what I do more seriously than I do. Most of what is done on the Commodore, as it was explained to me some time back, was considered "smoke and beer" money earned from selling programs to magazines and small software companies by some programmers. But to this guy, I was planning to make working on Commodore a career. I was going to write articles, create programs, and sell them to the highest bidder for the rest of my life. However, I didn't get into the Commodore game until 1989, just when Commodore was beginning to start losing its position as front runner of the computer world; in order to do that I had to get serious and start analyzing my work more closely. Yeah, better late than never.

Back in the earlier days of my working on the Commodore, I thought I could never do a thing wrong. I could rap out a line of code or type up some article and put it out into the Commodore community and everyone would think it was the best thing since Billy Shakespeare and I wouldn't have to edit a single word. My first draft was my final draft. I have since then grown up a little and, as you can tell by this piece, that review, rewriting, and reviewing again, is a vital part of the writing as well as the programming process. There is always more work to be done.

In this article I try my best to show you who have read the first edition of Run/Stop-Restore how much I have grown as a writer, the intense value of exercising the writing process, and careful research, can become a giant asset to the whole of the piece. While reading, enjoy the report, but please check on how much the style changed after allowing ten years of constant practice and careful review can make something good even better. Thanks to great people like you, I am better at what I do now more than I have ever been, and it can only go up from here.

COMMODORE GAMES FOR GIRLS

I have been pestering the good men and women of the Commodore community at large to come up with a list of Commodore games that were gender specific aimed at girls and so far no one has come up with anything for me, so, in my usual calm and controlled manner, I set out on my own to look up what could be found for this subject.

My journey to find this information came to one stop, where all my information was answered and even, in some cases, described in detail as to how they work. This stop was to our local Commodore guru of the past who shall be known in this article as The Commodore Man. I knew that if anyone would have this information about the subject at hand, it would be him, and he delivered quickly with some he snapped off in a quick email to me.

According to CM, there were very few Commodore 64 games made with girls in mind, but two really stand out – Barbie's Dream Date and Barbie's Dream House. In Barbie's Dream Date, Barbie receives a call from Ken. There is even a few 8 bit images of Barbie answering the phone and talking to Ken. Ken asks Barbie out to whatever place is selected by the randomness of the game. It could be to the prom, on a picnic, to hang out at the swimming pool, a casual dinner, or whatever. The next step in the game is that Barbie has to go shopping for all the necessary items needed for whatever date has been selected by Ken. So, it's into the car and into town she goes to find the right store to shop at for the right date. For example, if Ken asked Barbie to go to the prom, then she would have to stop at a bridal and gown shop for the right dress and the proper purse. If the pool is selected, then Barbie has to go to the swim shop and get items like a swim suit, some flip flops, and maybe even a sun hat, and on it goes. The fun thing about the game is that Barbie is on a time limit and has to pick up the items needed before the timer runs out. If the player does not get all the items necessary for the date selected, then Ken calls again and tells Barbie that plans have changed and if she would like to go to whatever Ken says it is. This means that the player has to start all over again and shop for the right items to match the date. However, if Barbie gets all the items necessary within the allotted time, then there is a picture of her and Ken on the date. Whoopie! Also, as another quirk, if Barbie picks up the wrong item, like a pair of flip flops for a prom dress, then Ken calls and changes plans also. CM points out that there seems to be no limit to how much money Barbie can spend at all the stores, like Barbie has direct access to the US Treasury.

In Barbie's Dream House, the player basically gets to design a home for her Barbie complete with room design and probably some furniture placing. The game is set up so that a user can use the game to design their own home, if one so wishes.

CM also pointed to a few other games that would best fit girls, like Mall Madness, where the user gets to go and buy things for their new home, which also includes getting a new car which I don't understand what that has to do with home décor. The Dating Game, which if anyone can remember how the TV show went, you already have what this game is about. Don't ask me, I didn't watch the show much – it interfered with my Star Trek watching, There is also The Love Boat, which is something I did watch because I was always interested in comedy, but the show was so mushy that I went back to watching my sci-fi programs, so I would guess that this game is about winning the heart of someone on the ship. There is My Pretty Pony, where the user is a pony and plays through a couple of simple adventures, or can even play dress up with their pony. This sounds more like a game for younger players who would be just discovering how to use the Commodore or any other computer of the time. Finally, there is My Dream Pet, where the user 'adopts' a virtual pet and takes care of it, something like the Tamagouchis that came out sometime in the late '90's. I remember watching people play these Tamagouchis while I was cleaning Metcalf South Mall back in the day. Even the mall manager had his own virtual pet and would spend hours at his desk playing with it. It's kind of neat to think that such a device was first started on a Commodore 64. My Dream Pet is the only iffy game that the Commodore Man mentions, since it could be gender neutral in its design, but this game is possibly too cutesy for boys, so he added it to the list of girl's games.

There are probably more Commodore games for girls, but these are the ones that CM could remember for me right off the top of his head and give me a decent description. I sure there are more within the confines of type in games and games to be found across the sea in countries like England and Germany, where Commodore stayed the top gaming system during the big Nintendo 8 bit bang that hit the United States, but they weren't in the great mind of the Commodore Man. To be honest, I was surprised to find that there were this many games for the Commodore 64 aimed specifically for girls. I did expect more, since Commodore was such a big system back in the day, but I guess that back then, to be market specific was not thought of at the time. Nowadays, such product is all over the place and divided into so many categories and sub-categories that they cannot be counted. However, when I walk into a game shop, like an EB Games or a Game Stop, I find things more focus for adults than kids, let alone girls. I guess that all of us who were gamers back in the 80's and 90's have grown up but we have not grown out of our love for video games. Now that I think about it, it is usually the guys in the game store while the girl friends wait outside the store and wither talk on the cell phone or spend that time texting other friends. Maybe I'm retarded, but I think that Commodore had the right idea of making something more gender specific, aiming at girls, than those who make video games now. I mean, there are few girls I know of that want to get into Modern Warfare 2 or Assassin's Creed 2, when they would rather be doing what girls like to do most – and don't ask me what that is, for I think that will still remain a mystery to the mind of man forever and ever.

THE NEW FAÇADE TO-
"A TYPICAL MEETING RUNDOWN"

Here within the lines of text in this piece is a cut from our Commodore magazine from Kansas City called Ryte Bytes. This section of the paper has been labeled The Last Word, which is usually found in the back of the newsletter. In The Last Word I attempt to give a play by play description of what happens in a typical Commodore meeting here in the Midwest. This meeting also ties in with my story about The Ledger and shows how a Commodore club goes about the task of helping me (and others who participate in programming) get a program down to where it will be useful for the average user of a 64. Within this piece you will find the progress of analysis in working with the program, suggestions, criticisms, helps, along with praise on the work at hand. As you will also read, there are not many attendees to such a meeting anymore since, quite obviously, interest in this style of computer is slowly on the wane. However, we few but proud still wave the Commodore banner high as we go forward into whatever is before us in the future. Commodore is fun for a lot of folk, and I am praying that as you read this book, you will understand why we hold on to such archaic merchandise. We who still hold the Commodore dear don't see it that way, but it is mainly the last vestige of when computers and people worked together instead of having computers do and think everything for us. One thing I have always been disappointed about today's computers is how much are given everything to do leaving people with little else but to sit back and watch as these machines, in whatever form they possess, take on the task meant for us. Maybe I just don't understand, but I do hope that you will see how The Ledger progresses in this piece from step to step into something more functional and user friendly.

A TYPICAL MEETING RUNDOWN

Last month the February newsletter went out electronically on its first real time run. Some of you received the January issue in the email as part of my trial to make sure this system works. Even though I have been doing this for some time, and that for just practice, and to see how well the magazine will be received through the email, there may have been some quirks that some users may not be able to handle, which makes it something I have to work on. Some of the complaints so far are:

"I can't open the files" – I will be directing these users to our website to where they can read the newsletter in the html format that Scott has set up there. This means that both Scott and I will have to get on the shtick and make sure the latest issue of the newsletter is there for downloading. I have to send Scott the Word documents that they are typed in and Scott will have to translate that to work on the website.

"I can read the second page through the first page" – This was a mess up on my part with the January issue as I sent a copy of the newsletter out through the .jpeg file and not using the original master copy, which is a single sheet at a time. Suggestions were made by users to put a black sheet of paper over the scanned sheet, thus eliminating the bleed through. I have gone back to using the master copy of the newsletter, which during the earlier months I have had no complaints.

"What kind of .jpeg file converter are you using?" - I am using my wife's Lexmark X74-X75 All in One machine and the software that comes with it. I scan the image into the scanner using the Black and White Photo option since using the Black and White Document makes for a very ugly and choppy image. This also makes for very small pages files. Dan Fisher, former Commodore user, gets these images and converts them to a sm.gif file that is sometimes less that 200K in size. If I don't have time to contact Mr. Fisher, I will send the .jpeg file as I convert it, which sometimes can get a large as 800K per page. With DSL and cable modems, this is not a problem, but there are some readers that still use standard 56K dial up, and these files take time to load. I try every month to get Mr. Fisher to convert the file, but as problems mount up at the Roach Hotel, I run out of time so I send the file at the .jpeg file size. I apologize for any inconvenience.

"Can you use a .pdf formatter?" – The Lexmark X74-X75 does have a format converter, but because of the size the document ends up in, which is larger that 10 megabytes, I cannot send the file through the email. I have tried. .Pdf is a better format the .jpeg I agree, but I need something that I know will work and can be sent through the email. I know that more modern Adobe Writers can make the grade and I need to take the time to search them out so I can get a better Adobe Creator and learn how to use same. If it is a simple as using the one in the Lexmark package, then I should learn in no time. Please be patient with me as I try to learn how to scan and covert the newsletter.

So how did it go for me in my first ever official electronic newsletter? First of all, let me say that I am still glad that I can use the Commodore to do this. One of the objections I had about using IBM and like computers to make the Commodore newsletter is that using said machine, I feel, does not make the newsletter Commodore. We are supposed to be Commodore users and to make everything on an IBM did not sound right. Making the newsletter with a Commodore machine and scanning into an image on an IBM makes up for some of what I was hoping for. We can still show readers what a Commodore can do and use the IBM machines to send it out to users of multiple formats and show off what our machine can do. Secondly, I still had to send the newsletter out in a paper format to some readers of our magazine. I thought that I would only have to make about six magazine letters but instead I found out that I made about thirteen of them for mailing in February. At the February meeting I got a couple of more email addresses but this is a far cry from the thirteen that I need to make the newsletter 100% electronic for both CUGKC members and clubs around the nation. I have already been informed that we have users that do not have Internet so I will be sending the paper out in the mail to them. Most of this problem has to do with me not remembering whose email I have and which club needs the paper version. I will have to work up a system that allows me to see who gets it electronically and who doesn't. Lastly there's still the timing issue. Most of this has to do with problems at the Hotel, but with prayer and time, I hope to do better in getting the newsletter out. Thanks be to God, I am improving. I just got the February issue of The Interface out before the February 28th deadline so things are getting done; it's just a matter of getting it done.

Now let's move onto the meeting ...

We had three in attendance at the February meeting: Jack, Gary, and I. Jack booted his trusty C64 and this time we got ourselves and decent image on the TV provided by the library. We quickly reviewed the latest issues of the 5C's disk which had a history of the Amiga computer on it and something about a quirk in the 1571 when reading and writing SEQ files on the second side of a 1571 formatted disk, which made no sense to me. I personally don't use the 1571 format on my 1571 disk drive. I always use the 1541 function on this machine since I don't have to worry about this problem. Since for the first few years of the Commodore 64's existence we used the 1541 disk drive, flipping a disk to access side two became second nature to a user.

We then took time out to peruse the next version of The Envelope Addressor which is called TEA 4 2. I took people around the parts of the program, showing its different functions and what they do, and we even took time out to read the credits that I put at the end of the pages. We also looked at the TEA.4.2.DOX file I wrote to explain the functions of TEA 4 2 and how I set that up in BASIC 2.0 using nothing more than PRINT statements. I wrote the documentation for TEA in the same format. How Reverend Moorman converted the program into a readable text that was cooperative with his set up is beyond me. The only comments I got was from Jack, who said in such great wisdom, "Who's going to use this?" I have to admit, he was right. With everything going electronic it would seem that TEA 4 2 is somewhat of a moot program. I use the program a lot in mailing out newsletters and I am planning on starting a second disk that will have my bills listed on it. Call me paranoid, but I like the idea of sending off a check in the mail that I know that I have written, examined and found correct, and put personally in the mailbox along with its corresponding invoice. Also, with LoadStar out of the Commodore scene, it would seem there is nowhere for me to present the program, or even its text, anywhere. I was planning on showing the program at some conventions, like I did when I went to the Las Vegas Expo, but with money quickly diminishing out of the coffers of the Roach Hotel, any trips would be considered as non fundable. It was suggested by Robert Bernardo of the Fresno group that I should consider sending a note to the editor/publisher of Commodore

Free magazine and see if he would be interested in putting the text of the program into it. I still have to check and see if he is interested.

What is slated for the March meeting?

Along with discussions of the latest Commodore magazines and disks that come into the Hotel to be brought to the meeting, I was going to have the attending body look over a work I have done over 10 years ago, provided I can find a working copy of it, called "Check File Creator/Editor" and give me some constructive criticism. This program was to be a companion to the 1992 release in RUN magazine called "Check It Out," but by the time the work was done RUN magazine had already closed its doors and there was no where to go with the program. That proved to be a blessing in disguise since I don't think the program was ready to run anyway. You should see some of the changes that RUN made to "Check It Out" before they published it in the magazine. My version I mailed in and the one I have here at the Hotel are almost two different programs. The programs do the same, but they show different things. Such is the prerogative of doing a work for hire by the ones buying the work. Anyway, the present version of "Check File ..." could use some work, like a new title. "Check File Creator/Editor" is a tad bit long. Yes, it describes what the program does in a sentence, but I don't feel as though the program should have a one sentence title. After sitting on the work for 10 years, I have come to the forgone conclusion that a better title for the work is "Check Mate." This tells the user that the program is made to be a companion to the "Check It Out" program, and therefore should function in conjunction with "Check It Out." We will see what can be done with it at the March meeting.

In April, Lord willing, I will bring a copy of "Check It Out" in its paper format as found in RUN magazine and also the copy that I wrote and sent off to the magazine. As for May, that is anybody's guess. I asked Dan Fisher for some help in coming up with programs and games to review, but he has been out of Commodore for a while and therefore cannot help me. Sure, he has some Commodore things on CD-R that is downloadable in WINVice, but he no longer has access to a 1581 or 1571 disk drive that allows these programs to be made Commodore ready. If anyone out in the Commodore community has some interesting programs that would be worthy of showing to the CUGKC, then please send me a copy of the program so I can show it at a CUGKC meeting. I personally am looking for a copy of the 1989(?) RUN magazine game, "Ketchup Attack." This is a cute and fun shoot-em-up wherein a space bound ketchup bottle tries to defend the galaxy from attacking burgers and fries trying to invade us.

With all that said, I guess that it is time that I end this long note in the pages of Ryte Bytes and save some things for the next issue. Please remember, if you are getting this magazine in the mail, I would prefer to send it to you in the email. Please send me your email address so I can add it to the Newsletter Recipients section. If you still need to get it in snail mail, then please let me know by mailing me at the address listed in the preceding paragraph. I would like to go for 100%, even though I am sure that this might not happen. After all, there are some die hard Commodore fans out in cyberspace that will not use anything else but a Commodore, even though there are comparable programs that run Commodore (like WINVice) that can be found on IBM, Macintosh, and the like.

THE NEW FAÇADE TO – "WRITER'S BLOCK OVER A NEWSLETTTER"

Writers block is a serious condition that seems to settle once in a while over a person whose job it is to write something. When I wrote this article I was facing both writers block and a deadline on getting something out for the paper. Things like this drive me nuts when it happens but one thing I have learned to during such situations is to just plow right on through. Usually this is a bad idea and one should just walk off for a while, do something else, and come back to the project later. I feel that sometimes a person just needs to barrel through it and just keep pressing the keys on the Commodore until something comes out. There is always the delete key to erase any unwanted words or phrases that you may have typed. This is how this piece was written. I just started typing in whatever came to mind and the next thing I knew I had an article about Commodore writers block.

This also happens when one is writing a Commodore program. Usually a programmer thinks he or she has everything needed in mind to make a program work, then goes about assembling the subroutines to make same. Once things are done, the beta test is initialized and the next thing you know a flood of information comes back saying that the program needs this or a subroutine is not working properly, or the evilest of demons – the program crashed. This is where a great users group comes in handy. They can give you necessary suggestions without exactly smashing your emotions into ashes, but I have been always told by more than one person: If you don't have a thick enough skin to handle the negative criticism that will come when you put things down in print, then get out of the business now before you get seriously hurt.

WRITER'S BLOCK OVER
A NEWSLETTER

What to write about.....

Did you ever get into that position? You sit down in front of your Commodore: the monitor is glowing brightly; the drive just finished loading up your favorite word processing program; you've got your favorite beverage sitting at arm's length from you, yet at a safe distance from your Commodore set up; waiting for something to pop into your head so you can jot down what has entered therein and -- nothing happens. When you're vocation or hobby is writing it is deplorable when writer's block sets in. You could possibly go insane if you can't come up with even a little something to fill a page. Even a sentence or two will give the avid writer some form of mental relief for a short time, but writers must continue to scribble. For those of us who have a passion for the art, it keeps us sane.

Billy Crystal's character in the film, "Throw Momma from the Train" said a line that was echoed throughout the movie, "A writer writes." Writes what? I don't know. That depends on who possess the word processor. For the versatile writer, no subject is taboo. If you write for a magazine or newsletter, like this one, you have the restrictions of staying within a certain confine, therefore your material must be within said confine, and in this case it is the Commodore 8-bit computer. I can't write about veterinary medicine and expect it to get published in the newsletter now, can I? But if I rewrite the same article and make it about how veterinary medicine and the Commodore work together, then we have something of interest to the readers of the newsletter.

Jack, in the June of 1999 issue of the newsletter asked for article submissions to the newsletter. I hope with this article to encourage you to try something like that. I don't think anyone is asking anyone else to be a Mark Twain or an Ernest Hemmingway, but just take a moment to express an anecdote about the Commodore. Many of us have been working on Commodores a long time. Write about some frustrations or accomplishments that are associated with your relationships to your machine. Also there are some new users among us. I would personally like to know why, or what sold you on getting a Commodore over an IBM or Macintosh and how they like their new addition to the family, and also if there are any problems we as a group can help you with.

For example of a problem, Frank came to me one meeting and asked if I could write some sort of a screen saver for the Commodore 64 and Commodore 128 models. I have deliberated and considered his idea for quite some time and in response wrote an article concerning his suggestion. I uploaded it to the Commodore BBS newsletter file section, but if I understood right, there was a problem in the transfer protocol I used and I needed to upload the article again using a different protocol. But the point I'm trying to make is that I did write the article and submitted it for the editor's approval despite the problems in sending the material over the phone line.

But what if the article is bad? What if nobody likes it? If that's what's keeping you from sending something to the newsletter then my suggestion to you is: STOP THINKING THAT WAY!! My experience has taught me there is always at least one person who will appreciate what you have written out of the multitudes that thinks your work is garbage. They may wish they would have done it themselves or they are grateful that you made this point of subject known. Maybe you made them laugh and put a spot of sunshine in their otherwise dreary day. Sometimes you'll never know if you've touched someone either positively or negatively, but you'll never know if you don't try. My dad told me that trying and failing is better than going through life never trying and wondering what the results would have been. I wouldn't be where I am today if it wasn't for me trying and failing; and getting up only to try again. Kind of like that falling off the proverbial horse thing. Yeah, you know what I'm talking about.

If you wish to give an article a try but want somebody to check it over before it goes to the editor, then leave me a message in the "Club -Talk" echo on the Commodore B.B.S. then upload your article to the "General Info" area of the file sections.

That's it! Get those Commodore word processing packages loaded and start typing. Remember this as you start writing: The longest story starts with the first letter, of the first paragraph, on the first page.

THE NEW FAÇADE TO-
"THE RISE AND FALL OF THE PULPIT"

This is one of the new stories added to Run/Stop-Restore: 10th Anniversary Edition. I was asked one day by the Late Lord Ronin, "Whatever happened to your BBS?" I was going to answer him in a short letter, but the creative juices of my mind started to unravel a story based explanation as to the reasons of how the BBS came into existence and how it came to a slow and steady end. This is the most published story I have written to date with the piece being first issued in the Astoria Commodore Users Group's magazine, The Village Green, and later the story found its way into the international magazine Commodore Free, and now here it is presented in this book. I dedicate this story to Lord Ronin of ACUG who with just a simple question sent to me in an email made me begin to think of all the times I had putting the BBS together, finding the right software, collecting the hardware, getting a new phone line put in the works. Except for the fictional opening and closing of the article, everything in it happened just as it was written. There is no way I could have come up with something as weird as what transpired for me back in those days, so it had to be true.

This was a fun story to write and even better to think up. The opening line was taken from a Commodore program offered on RUN magazine which was a book creation program that I never got to use. The magazine even offered a prize for the best story submitted. The reward was some cash and a chance to be published on a Commodore disk using the book reading program to read the winner's story. I tried to get into this but I had nothing written so I never tried. This program was a prelude to the electronic books that are out now. I am finding out one thing about the computer world, what we see now was more than likely done twenty or so years ago on a Commodore.

THE RISE AND FALL OF THE PULPIT

It was a dank and clammy night. The wind wafted through the trees, obliterating any light being made by the moon. I stood in the empty alley behind the 7-11 awaiting … him. He was late. I should of known better than to trust him, but he was the only one who had the goods. Sure, I could have gone out of town and picked it up, but I was already running late. A trip out of town would require a "special" explanation to the wife, and I have lied to her enough. After this last pick up, I would be done. I'm calling it quits. I'm getting too old and the people I have been dealing with are becoming too dangerous.

Just as I was ready to give up, get back into my '85 Chevette, and leave, I heard him. Who couldn't hear him? His old '76 Toyota Corolla with the bad muffler bearing and squeaky shocks could be heard from a quarter mile away. As he approached, the alley cats scrambled for cover. I should have done the same, but this meeting was too important, and I needed his "special" brand of merchandise.

His one headlight remained on high beam as he stopped just behind my car and his vehicle sputtered to a stop. I could barely see the driver, but I knew it had to be … him. The moan of a rusty car door opening, the crunch of gravel under foot, and the rhythmic footfalls told me that he was approaching. He stopped just in front of his headlight, the light silhouetting his frame. His appearance was that of nothing I have ever seen.

He was a ball. That's right. Nothing more than a ball, perfectly round hairy ball of … what? My contact looked like a five foot tribble as he slowly approached me.

"Captain L?" he asked in a gruff voice.

"The same." I tried looking past the fuzz, but to my amazement I didn't find anything tangible that was holding this hairball up. "Am I addressing The Great Hairy One?"

"At your service," he replied.

"Do you have the stuff?" I asked directly.

"Do you have the payment?"

I patted my left jacket pocket. "I have it here."

"Let's see it."

"First let me see the merchandise."

"Don't you trust me?"

"I trust everyone. It's the devil inside them I don't trust."

"Do you think I'm the devil?"

I looked intently at him. "I don't know what to think. Nonetheless, the merchandise, please."

The Great Hairy One grunted. I think it was a laugh, but from the creature I could not tell. He stepped to the rear of his Toyota and somehow opened the trunk.

"Come and see," he beckoned.

I stepped out of the headlight beam and crossed to the back of his Toyota, my body tense and ready for anything. This unknown creature could do anything and without me knowing where any hands, feet, or weapons would hide I didn't want to take any chances. I stood at the back of the car for a few minutes, waiting for my eyes to adjust to the little lighting that was there, but once they did, I could not believe what I was looking at …

There before me was all that I was looking for … Commodore drives, keyboards, REUs, modems, the whole lot.

"I brought extra in case there was something else that you wanted," The Great Hairy One said.

I started to rummage through the plethora of Commodore computer equipment when something grabbed my arm and pulled me back. I looked at The Great Hairy One. He was standing close.

"Tsk, tsk," he said gruffly. "You've seen that I deliver, now how about you?"

I reached into my left jacket pocket and pulled out a flat, plastic, square package. Something from under the fuzz pulled it out of my hand and the package was instantly consumed by the hair. He began to giggle; at least I think it was a giggle. At any rate, I think he was happy with what I brought in exchange for the Commodore merchandise.

"Weird Al's 'Even Worse' album on CD," he said, "just what I asked for, and new, too."

"I got it fresh off of this thing called Amazon. I never opened it. I brought it immediately out here to you."

"You've done well." There was a lilt in his voice.

"Please feel free to take all that you need."

"Do you want something extra for the other Commodore stuff?"

"I already have all I wanted," The Great Hairy One said as the sound of the first track began to play from underneath all the hair. I quickly rummaged through the computer equipment, grabbed an extra 1581 drive, an REU, and some DSDD 3.5 disks and made my way back to my Chevette. After loading these items in the car, I got in, started the vehicle and left. All the while The Great Hairy One was dancing away around the alley…

Thus was the beginning of the work which was soon to become the greatest and yet short lived bulletin board system ever to run on a Commodore 64 … the Pulpit BBS.

Well, this may not be **exactly** how this all began … in fact, this is only partly true … all right, I lied out my teeth! You want the truth? Fine, I'll give it to you, but I must warn you, it's not anywhere as exciting or mysterious as the previously written pages.

It began in the summer of 1994. I was calling so many local BBS' from my Commodore and even though all these boards were great, there really didn't seem to be anything out there for anyone of faith to call that was

Commodore based. I have seen how some of these boards were set up from my calling in and the jealously began to rage in my breast. I know I could do something better with my C64 system, but I had neither practical experience nor the software to make it all possible. On a perchance posting on the "KBPD" Commodore board, I read from its SysOp, "Sgt. Butch," that he was planning to shut down his board in favor of going to the IBM format and was looking for someone to purchase his Commodore equipment and subsequent files which made up the "KBPD." I instantly jumped at this opportunity and after several hours on my knees begging my beautiful and understanding wife Alana to allow this purchase to take place, we were on our way to Belton, Missouri, with money in hand and her father's pick up to get this large amount of Commodore merchandise. The deal was struck, and within about an hour's time we had all of "Sgt. Butch's" Commodore computers, drives, and disks loaded in the Dodge Ram and we headed back to Kansas City, Kansas.

"It's your stuff, dear," Alana said sternly as we pulled up in front of the house. "You drag it into the house and put it away. I want nothing more to do with it."

Like a child in a candy store, I began the joyous task of unloading the pick-up and putting all that Commodore equipment in its proper place. As I dragged all this out of the vehicle, I examined each piece carefully, deciding what could go into storage in the basement and what went immediately into the computer room for set up to my soon to exist BBS. As I worked a thought occurred to me: What was I going to call my new BBS? Sure, it was going to be set up as a Christian BBS, but it needed a catchy name … something that would grab a user's attention and make him keep coming back for more. Should it be called "The Church, The Steeple, The Way, The Door, or The Outhouse?" I finally had to begin to analyze what it was I was going to do… bring the gospel of Jesus Christ to many wayward Commodore users throughout the greater Kansas City area and beyond. Therefore, by the time everything had a place the name was chosen. Where else does one hear about the Word but from the pulpit? So by set up time, the new BBS was going to be named The Pulpit.

Now, what software was I going to use? I had "Sgt. Butch's" C*Base 3.0 disk, but with working offline with the confusing and often frustrating C*Base 2.0, I wasn't ready to tackle its upgraded cousin. I went through the disk files and found several BBS packages to work with. After calling several friends, I asked them to call in to my house line with their Commodores and go through each BBS package I uploaded and give me their opinion of each. One by one, packages like Ivory and other programs, both familiar and unfamiliar, were eliminated. Finally, the argument was inevitable. I had to learn to use C*Base 3.0, the best BBS package for the Commodore 64 of the day.

I dialed into "The Temple of Doom" BBS and asked its SysOp, "Indiana Jones," who was running C*Base 3.0, for a crash course in how to set up and operate the software. He was very cordial and helped me in ways I couldn't imagine. It took a couple of weeks, but I got all the files ready and each disk drive set up to receive messages in accordance to the functioning of C*Base.

The day came. I posted on all the BBS' I was a member of to let users know that The Pulpit BBS was online and ready to help in any spiritual needs out there in cyberspace. At first the calls came rushing in, so much so that we put in a second phone line to handle the flow of messages and questions. Then the BBS went from part time to a full 24/7 running time. At first it seemed that The Pulpit was going to be a big success and everything was going to be fine. What could possible go wrong?

Plenty.

I'm sure those who ran BBS' in the past have had their share of "rascals" that would log in and start harassing the users. The Pulpit had its "problem child." A Ku Klux Klan member who liked to call in at 3:00 am while drunk and send hate messages to everyone on the board began causing stuff among members. Distress posts went out to me and I tried to quell those who were distressed by letting them know that The Pulpit, like a church, was open to all those who are in need. It was apparent that this person was in need and I didn't want to "shut him out of the church" because he had a problem. That would not show him the help he seemed to need. However, I would "talk" with him and see what could be done. Our conversation was brief in the message base, but the user agreed to back off and not do that again. A week went by and everything was fine. Then a post came to me saying he was getting sexually rude with one of the women members of the BBS. I went into the private message base of The Pulpit and read what was sent to one of the women. Nothing shocking in my opinion, but still I would investigate further. The "problem" user again agreed to back off.

Keeping this person as a user on The Pulpit and not just "kicking him out" like other users insisted I should do began to draw off members to the BBS. Calls became more infrequent to the base. I would check on some of the other BBS where I knew some of these users frequented and they all basically said that if you're going to keep that "person" around on The Pulpit, then they were not going to call in anymore. I finally demoted this user's access rating to the lowest possible, leaving him a private message explaining what I had done and why. A heated message came back from him and he no more called The Pulpit. I posted on the other BBS' that the problem was permanently solved, but the damage was already done. If this was how I was going to conduct my "church," then they wanted no part of it. Calls came almost to a crawling halt. The Pulpit was dying.

To add insult to injury, one summer day in July 1995, I got a knock on my living room door while I was working on some upload files to The Pulpit. I got up and answered the door. Before me stood a uniformed member of the Kansas City, Kansas Police Department and a worker from the Board of Public Utilities. The officer spoke first.

"Are you Lenard Roach?"

"I am," I answered. "Is there something wrong?"

"May we come in?"

"Surely," I said. I stepped away from the door and allowed the officer and BPU worker into the house. The officer stood in front of me while the worker immediately went about the house checking in each room. He entered the basement where I stored all of the Commodore overflow.

"What is this all about, officer?" I asked. At first I thought that maybe my dog bit a BPU worker while they were out to read the meter and they were searching for the dog, but the officer's words brought me to a total loss.

"Mr. Roach, are you aware that you are using a lot of energy at this residence?"

"No." Now I thought someone tapped into my power again, but the officer continued to speak.

"Mr. Roach, we have reason to believe that something illegal is happening in this house."

My jaw dropped. "Like what?" I asked.

"You tell me."

"I have no idea." I pointed to the basement. "What does something illegal have to do with the BPU?"

"Mr. Roach," the officer began, "whenever the Board of Public Utilities detects a spike in energy use, they call us to come out with them to examine the premises in case they find any illegal activity. With their diligence we have shut down many operations here in the area."

"What kind of illegal operations might I ask?"

"Portable pot farms."

I drew a breath in amazement. "Are you trying to say that I have been growing marijuana here and the BPU can detect that? How is that possible?"

"Portable pot farms require a lot of sunlight in order to make them work. This sunlight can be artificially created with sunlamps put in a damp spot like a basement or crawl space where marijuana can grow and thrive. Sunlamps need a lot of electricity to work. This excess energy use causes a spike in the customer's electricity bill, drawing suspicion that the resident may be doing something illegal. When that happens, they call us and we come out with the BPU to investigate."

"So you think I'm growing pot, right?"

"Again, you tell me."

The BPU worker came up from the basement and crossed the kitchen into the dining room where the officer and I were.

"I didn't find anything here that looks like they had any sunlamps hooked up to anything in the basement or crawl space."

The officer looked square at me. "Can you explain the spike in energy use in your home, Mr. Roach?"

I turned to the BPU worker. "May I ask when your department detected the so called 'energy spike' in my bill?"

"About six months ago," he answered.

"That's about the same time I set up this." I led the men to the computer area where I was working earlier on The Pulpit. I pointed at the Commodore 64. "I have been running an online BBS that is like an electric church. Would you like to see how it works?"

"That's not necessary," the officer said. The BPU worker got on his hands and knees and looked at all the power bricks that went to the keyboard and various drives of the unit. After a few seconds of examination, he arose and faced the officer.

"This has to be it," he said. "These components are each pulling a significant amount of power. Put them all together and you have an good power drain."

I smiled at them both. Really, I was trying to keep a civil tongue in my mouth by not shouting "Retards!" directly to their faces.

The officer sighed and hung his head for a moment. He looked up at me and also smiled. "We're sorry to have bothered you, Mr. Roach. Please understand that this is all a routine. Please accept our apologies. You have a nice day. We'll see ourselves out."

After the officer and BPU worker left, I sat down in the computer chair and faced the Commodore 64; a rude user, no callers, and now this. I looked up at the ceiling to address God. "I'm sorry, sir," I said, "This just isn't worth it." I hopped online and posted at several different boards that The Pulpit was going to close its "doors" by the end of next week. "Thanks for everyone's support in this endeavor, but I feel it necessary that due to circumstances this ministry should shut down." I got some "congratulations for a job well done", and some "sorry to see it leave" messages on the other boards, but nothing came to The Pulpit's boards directly. By the end of the week, I pulled the plug on what once started as a great idea.

Six months passed...

"Lenard, what are you going to do with all this Commodore junk?" Alana asked in January of 1996. "If you're not going to do that computer thingie that you were so hopped up to do last year, then do something with all this stuff."

She was right. All I was using my Commodore for now was writing, BBS calling, and the occasional game play. I needed to clear some of this equipment out of the office and put it somewhere other than the basement, where the load of "Sgt. Butch's" Commodore machines and disks still remained. My glory days of making my Commodore out to be something were all gone. As a matter of fact, with the introduction of this thing they were calling the "internet," BBS were shutting down by the dozens. There really wasn't much thinking about what should be done. The Commodore was still great, but there can still be too much of a good thing. This was it. I stepped over to the phone and made a call…

It was a clear and cold night. I awaited by my Chevette for … his … arrival behind the 7-11. I didn't have to wait long to hear the familiar sputtering of the Toyota. Behind me he parked and got out. The five foot fuzz ball that was The Great Hairy One stepped out of his vehicle and approached me.

"Your post said this was something worth my time," he said in his gravelly voice. "What have you got?"

I opened the hatchback of the Chevette and showed him the plethora of Commodore hardware, disks and magazines I loaded up before the trip. He examined the merchandise carefully.

"I remember a post you made to 'The Temple of Doom' BBS some time back saying that you would love to have gotten your hands on whatever 'Sgt. Butch' had hidden in his garage that he wouldn't sell to you. He sold it all to me and here it is."

If he had eyes, I think they would have brightened by then. "You're kidding?" he asked me. "This is 'Sgt. Butch's Commodore stash?"

I nodded. He literally jumped into the tail of the car and started digging through the material like a ravenous beast. I stepped back to stay away from any flying debris as he pushed away hardware and software to find the bits he always wanted. His fur, like "tentacles," was holding several pieces of software and equipment in the air.

"This is glorious," he said. "I heard rumor that he had this stuff, but I could never see it for myself. Some of this stuff will give me a pretty penny on the open market. How much to you want for the lot?"

"Nothing, It's all yours."

The material he was "holding" fell to the ground. I think he was staring at me in disbelief.

"I can't do that, Captain," he said. "It wouldn't be right. I've got to give you something for a haul like this."

"You'd be doing me a favor by just taking it off my hands," I said. "It's starting to clutter up the basement anyway. You'd be making the wife and I very happy if you would take it."

The Great Hairy One took a step forward. "Captain, I'm really sorry about what happened to The Pulpit. It's a great loss to the BBS community. You know I enjoyed visiting your board, but that's no reason to be giving all this stuff away. Please let me give you something for it."

"Like what?"

From under a tuft of fuzz came a crisp $50 bill.

"Take it," he said. "Consider it a final donation to a once worthy ministry."

I hesitated for a moment then I reached out and took the money and stared at it. Already The Great Hairy One was loading all the equipment into his Toyota. In mere moments, the Chevette was empty and his car was full.

I climbed into the Chevette and awaited The Great Hairy One to pull out so I could leave, but instead he met me at the driver's door.

"Captain," he said, "thanks for everything."

I reached out and petted his massive hair. "Thank you."

"What will you do now?"

"Don't you worry," I said as I started the engine, "I'm not out of the Commodore business yet. I've got one program published and I'm working on another. A sequel, who knows? Maybe I'll write a book about working on the Commodore. I don't think anyone's ever done that."

"Give me a copy."

"Better than that, I'll let you proofread it and I'll put whatever comments you have about it on the back of the book."

"Done."

With that, The Great Hairy One got into his vehicle, backed out, and left, leaving me to ponder my Commodore future ...

THE NEW FAÇADE TO-
"... AND NOW FOR SOMETHING DIFFERENT ..."

I love to write as it is apparent from looking upon this upcoming article. Back in the days I used to write programs on the Commodore just so I could write the documentation, hoping that the documentation would somehow outsell the program. Silly me. One of the reasons why I created the Pulpit was to start a particular subboard, as well as try to get the message of salvation in Jesus Christ out to the computer world. I was told by the person who led me into the BBS gig that if my BBS did not contain an adult subboard of some kind, then my board would not be successful. "Nobody wants to hear about religion on the computer," she told me, "so you're just setting yourself up to fail." I so wanted to prove her wrong, but as her adult oriented BBS flourished, my Christian BBS floundered and died. Life can hand you a hard deal sometimes, even when it comes to serving Jesus, but all you can do is get up, brush yourself off, and try again. Elsewhere in the book I describe the Pulpit in great detail, and the conflicts that helped bring it to a quick demise.

The upcoming article is an extraction from the Pulpit BBS that I ran back in the early 90s, right on the edge of the introduction of the Internet to the world. I tried several attempts to get this board started off right, but nothing seemed to be clicking with my visitors, so I finally settled on a Perry Mason style situation, which gave me the most hits to the subboard. I have been asked by a few people to flourish this story line into a actual book, which might make for a good project sometime in the future, but for now please sit back and enjoy reading this wonderful piece from days gone by.

AND NOW FOR
SOMETHING DIFFERENT

This time I decided that a little change of pace might be in order. I tapped into the files of one of the sub boards on the Pulpit and came up with a sample of what is occurring on the BBS. This particular sub is entitled the RPG, or (R)ole (P)laying (G)ame; but before we begin I believe that a few explanations might be in order.

First of all, this is a Christian BBS from where this information came from; this means there will be a lot of religious overtones, undertones, and directness. For those who finds such things offensive, I'm sorry that you are; but this material was removed from a Christian based BBS. No relationship of what is published here has any relation to the Commodore Users Group or any of its subsidiaries or their views.

Also, some spelling and usage of verbs may sound rough, but as stated beforehand, this is a direct transcript from a Pulpit sub board. Part of the job of the participants to the sub is to be as clever as they can with the last group of posts entered and still try to keep or change the flow of the main storyline.

Now with all that said, on to the posts at hand:

SUBJECT: Let's Try This Scenario
POST #: 1
USER: Captain L!
DATE: 5/28/95
TIME: 12:39 AM

It is a typical day at the business offices of the Pulpit. Captain L is busy studying the scriptures and getting ready for whatever may come his way today. Ladybug is busy out front typing away at the last reports received from their last case -- a small misunderstanding of the word, quickly cleared up and no one hurt. As a matter of fact, a new person claimed Jesus as Savior out of that deal. Good profit. SuperBug is doing what he does best, lounging about on the office sofa, using the one arm rest as a pillow and the other to elevate his feet, daydreaming of some girl at school he's been swooning over for the past two months. He pushes his sunglasses onto his forehead and glances over at the studious Captain L.

"Cap," he begins, "how in the world could someone just miss out on something like our last client did? I mean, even I knew that and I'm just a kid!"

"It's not too hard," Captain L replies, not looking up at the SuperBug. "Sometimes we get torn up about something that happens and forget that God really loves us despite what is happening in our lives at the moment. We just have to trust him even though things are getting a little hot for us. His Spirit says dwells within us; both the letters to the Galatians and Ephesians says that. He helps us through by bringing to mind God's word and leads us when the way grows a little dark to see."

"Well, at least we got our client back onto the right track again, and her husband got saved along the way."

"Amen," Captain L said, finally looking up over his Bible. "Their situation hasn't changed, but their outlook on it has."

"Captain L," comes Ladybug's voice over the desk intercom, "there's a very large gentlemen here to see you and he looks like he's not..."

Just then the door to Captain L's office flings open with a tremendous crash. Such forced is used that the upper hinge snaps off and the door becomes instantly embedded into the wall. The bust of the apostle Paul, which resides on a mahogany stand opposite the door frame falls to the floor, smashing into dust; in strolls a very tall, hugely built, angry man wearing a hat and raincoat; totally a different dress from the sunny day happening outside. He storms over to Captain L's desk with Ladybug on his heels. He stops at the desk and smashes his fists into the table top, burying his hands up to his wrists. He stares demonized at the now standing Captain L!

"...Very happy," Ladybug finally gets to conclude.

SuperBug is well past off the sofa and already hovering between the floor and the ceiling waiting with arms cocked back for anything more hostile from the obviously dangerous intruder.

Captain L smiles.

"Can I help you, sir?"

"Captain L" bellows the big man in a deep, reverberating voice, "I've had it with you and your meddling!! This time you're gonna pay!!"

SUBJECT: Continued
POST#: 2
DATE: 5/29/95
TIME: 9.21 PM

"I didn't even know that I was in debt. With what collection agency are you working for? Perhaps...."

But before the Captain could finish, the hostile giant spins around and grabs Ladybug around the waist with one hand. By lifting her off the ground, he hurls the beautiful Ladybug past the SuperBug and through the plate glass window that faces toward the city.

"You moron!" screams SuperBug. "We're fifteen stories up!" Without a further thought, SuperBug flies out the window after the falling Ladybug.

Captain L focuses his attention back to the hulk like gentleman, making sure his steel blue eyes comes in contact directly into the space on the being where he should have his. "That was totally uncalled for, sir," says Captain L in a stern tone. "I command you in the name of Jesus to tell me who you are!"

"Back off, Cap! I got him!" comes a shout from across the room. SuperBug has already brought Ladybug back into the room and laid her on the sofa the same way he was lying earlier. He also placed a wet cloth on her forehead.

"SuperBug! Stop!" screams the Captain, but it's too late. SuperBug already is flying what short distance there was between the monster and himself, his fists glowing with Samson-like strength that will surely knock out a charging rhino. The stranger swats SuperBug out of the air as though he was some annoying insect. His body goes limp as he crashes through two office walls and into the hallway outside. Cap jumps out from behind his desk and speeds through the open doors into the hall to check on the young superhero now slumped against the hall wall next to the water fountain, unconscious.

Captain L wastes no time in filling his hands with water from the fountain and splashing it into the face of the SuperBug. After a couple of baptisms in the face with the Freon cooled water, SuperBug regains consciousness.

"Ladybug...." SuperBug stutters weakly.

"Nuts!" exclaims Captain L. In his haste to help Superbug, he quickly forgot about Ladybug and goes back into the office area where he found nothing but a demolished office that he first left. Ladybug is still lying on the sofa, also regaining consciousness; but the large, powerful behemoth is nowhere to be found.

Captain L steps over to Ladybug and helps her to a sitting position. "I'll call for the elders of the church," Captain L says while digging through the rubble for a phone.

"That won't be necessary, Cap," Ladybug says in a weak, but sweet voice, "I'll be all right."

"Me, too," says SuperBug as he walks back into the office while rubbing the back of his head and neck. He sits down next to Ladybug. "That guy was powerful," he continues. "Got any idea who he was, Cap?"

"A calling card," Captain L answers. "I think we've just been warned by the powers of darkness that we've got a little too close to their operations around here and they are telling us to back off."

"Some telling!" exclaims SuperBug.

"What are you going to do?" asks Ladybug. "Are you going to back off?"

"I don't give in to threats," Captain L answers with a flash in his eyes," but I also don't like the idea of my friends getting hurt at my expense. Why don't you two go down to Windjammer's marina and stay in one of his houseboats he has docked there? I'll deal with this one myself."

"No chance, Captain L!" says SuperBug. "I'm in for the duration. Besides," he adds smiling, "I owe this clown one."

"I'm in, too," chimes Ladybug.

"It's going to be dangerous," the Captain says to his friends.

"Let's get going," says the energized SuperBug.

"What's our first move, Captain L?" says Ladybug.

"First thing to do is contact all the members of the Pulpit. I think we're going to need their help."

"I'm on it," Ladybug says while stepping to her desk.

"Me, too," echos SuperBug as he flies out the window.

Captain L looks over this office.

"The second thing," he says to himself," is to fix this office back up."

SUBJECT: Daimon the Mentally Challenged
POST#: 3
USER: Northern Lights BBS
DATE: 6/25/95
TIME: 3:43 AM

Then came Daimon, the mentally challenged fellow and he walks up to the Pulpit and his Depend diaper was saturated with urine and his clothes are all wet because no one told him to come out of the rain because he is a dullard....."

SUBJECT: Continued
POST#: 4
USER: Captain L!
DATE: 7/13/95
TIME: 11:50 AM

"Daimon," says Captain L! "you're one of SuperBug's operatives, aren't you?"

"Yes," he says. "He told me he would be here."

"You just missed him. He's off to contact the rest of the Pulpit members. It seems we've had a visitor. I'll fill you in as you get out of that diaper and into some clothes SuperBug leaves here for just such an occasion. I think you'll find my story interesting."

Captain L chats away about the events of the last half hour while Daimon Maximillion changed into the silk tweed suit that waited on the other side of the library door. Soon Daimon steps from behind the door and sits in the straight back chair facing the splinter pile that used to be Captain L's desk.

"That's quite a tale," Daimon comments at the end of the story. He looks around the room. "And this is quite a mess."

"It'll take some time to clean up, but it's nothing the Lord can't help us do. Will you assist us in tracking down this visitor of mine?"

"Consider it done," Daimon says as he rises and begins to step out of the office. Captain L's voice stops him short.

"Tell me one thing before you leave, please."

"Sure."

"Why were you in that weird getup?"

Daimon hesitates. "SuperBug had me staking out a day care facility that was under suspect of using the children as part of some satanic ritual. I tried to go in as an infant. I stood outside trying to soil my Depends just for effect."

"Aren't you a little big for that?"

"Hey, anything for the cause of Jesus, I figure. Then it started to rain. It must have been a microburst because the whole area was soaked but I see that your block is nice and dry. Anyway, while all of this was happening, I saw someone who worked there sneak a baby out of the nursery and down the alleyway. I radioed ahead to the next operative to spot them and follow them on, which he is now doing. If this all turns out true, we were to contact SuperBug and let him make the bust since he has the super powers and all."

"Good work, Daimon," Captain L says. "Let me know what you find out on the visitor I had. God be with you."

"Amen," echoed Daimon and turns to leave only to meet Ladybug rushing into Captain L's office, waving a legal piece of paper in her hand...

As you can see, users are used as characters and users input their ideas and other users bounce off that idea, even if it takes off of the thought as a whole. If you think this is fun and would like to input your own ideas, then please call the Pulpit from 8 PM to 8 AM and challenge your imagination.

THE NEW FAÇADE TO- "WHAT'S GOING ON WITH THE PULPIT?"

It seems that when things begin to occur, it happens in droves. I remember living in the old house where this episode took place and having all this come down us while we struggled to get along with the situation. The house I am presently in as of this writing also had to have the wiring redone, but this house we are buying while the former house we were just renting.

Usually I would put such occurrences under the file "persecution for righteousness sake," but as you know everything happens for a reason and this little escapade of wiring was done to get the new house up to code – kind of like what happened to the old house. But nonetheless, as you can tell by reading, the Commodore BBS called the Pulpit was down and there was nothing I could do about it at the time.

This is another story about the adventures of the Pulpit BBS and some of obstacles we were facing while we had it up and running for the one year it was online. Like any other business, there were problems within and problems without. Other stories in this book will lead you to some of the problems within, but this is a story about problems without – problems we had absolutely no control over. The one big thing I did learn from running the Pulpit was the need I had to learn customer service skills and to also deal with the various kinds of people that would call in. This variety of folk helps made the world go around.

Remember those days, or weeks, or months, or maybe even years, in your life when things just didn't seem to go right? This story could be a reminder to you of what those circumstances were and how you eventually waded your way out of them. I was told something by a pastor a long time ago: You are either coming out of a storm of life, going into a storm of life, or you are in a storm of life. Let this story be that reminder. Enjoy.

WHAT'S GOING ON
WITH THE PULPIT?

Many changes have been happening with and around the Pulpit, but mostly around it. During the hot summer months the air conditioner plus the BBS would blow a fuse, so until the weather got cool enough to keep the AC off we had to keep the BBS off-line. As you know this would take almost a whole month the way the summer goes. Then we decided to clean the AC just to see if it was just the wiring of our old house or not. Come to find out there was plenty of dust and dirt trapped in there. It took short of $100 to clean it, but now we can run both the AC and the BBS again, but more trouble arose. Our last JiffyDOS keyboard bit the dust, so I had to downgrade the Pulpit to a C64 and a 1581 drive until repairs could be initialized. Repairs were completed, but the problems did not end there. Blowing all the fuses that the house did caused the outside lines to fry out, so out the electric company comes to fix it and while they were doing the necessary repair work decided to inspect the wiring and found our landlord to be in violation and gave him ten days to rectify our wiring or be shut down. Naturally, as most businessmen are who only wish money without putting out any cash, he waited and the electric company shut us down. Not him, us. Our food got quickly transferred to my parent's refrigerator in Olathe and the wait began for power to be restored. While we lived on lanterns, candles and flashlights the Pulpit remained down. Thanks be to God this was happening during a cool down time so nobody in my house was dying of heat stroke. Fearing a lawsuit from us our landlord instantly began work on repairing and upgrading our electrical system according to the electric company standards, which got final approval around the middle week of September, and power was reinitialized to the house and has been there ever since.

Please don't take this tale as a weeps and woes story. I've been granted this opportunity by the newsletter to tell those who regularly use the Pulpit where it has been for the good parts of August and September, which basically it has been fighting the moronics of both sysop and the sysop's landlord. But right now the BBS is back on line and running at its full 100 Megs.

Please feel free to call anytime between 8pm and 8am, 7 days. I would love to hear from all who read this article. I pray I have something on the Pulpit for all of you.

THE NEW FAÇADE TO – "PROGRAM WHERE ARE YOU?"

I remember working on this piece. I just wanted to see what it would look like if you took the average Commodore user and your average Commodore computer, put them on a stage and gave them a chance to perform in front of a live audience. I just took my experiences with the machine at various times of my using it and put it all into one little act that took no more than five minutes to do. The fun of this was that I was just about to write one day an actual three act play based on an average 80s household getting a Commodore and all the problems, as well as fun, that they would have by actually setting it up and using it and I was going to use the stories found in Run/Stop-Restore as a basis. I was on my way until I abandoned the project for reasons still unknown.

In either case as you read this please understand this is an exaggeration of what could actually happen when a person starts using a Commodore. Most of these ideas are not an actual problem, in fact, I found out that because I never have used a brand new machine (all of mine have been hand me downs), that I was just inheriting someone else's problems as to why they got rid of them. My wife at the time begged me to spend the extra $100 or so and get a new machine, just to get the feel of having one without difficulties, but my stubbornness and our lack of funds made it impossible for me to get a new one. For right now, and for the future, I will always be using the used units that are plentifully available at Commodore clubs and thrift shops found throughout the area.

Please enjoy the next selection and the lightheartedness that I have written it in.

PROGRAM, WHERE ARE YOU?
A Short Play In Less Than One Act

PLAYERS:

Your typical Commodore computer

Your atypical user

COMMODORE: Load"PRG",8,1

USER: Alright! Let's get going!

(USER leaves work station; orders pizza over phone; watches outrageous talk show. Pizza comes. Pays for and eats pizza; goes back to work station.)

COMMODORE: Loading...

USER: What the?

(USER checks drive and finds that it has locked up. Swaps drive.)

COMMODORE: Load"PRG",8,1

USER: Now let's see.

(USER leaves work station; watches soap opera; returns.)

COMMODORE: Insert copy of PRG version 1.5 or higher.

USER: What's this?

(USER refers to documentation which is written in a unknown tongue. USER goes to the library and gets a translator's dictionary; returns. Translates manual to the point where he can load program.)

USER: Now let's try.

(USER uses backup copy of PRG that comes in the software packet.)

COMMODORE: Load"PRG",8,1

USER: One more time....

(COMMODORE quickly boots and icons appear.)

USER: All right!

(USER tries to use mouse but it doesn't work; swaps mice. Still doesn't work. Translates manual some more. Removes mouse and inserts joystick into port. Arrow icon moves.)

USER: Yes!

(USER finds the icon marked joystick/mouse swap. Presses fire button. Icon moves.)

USER: Now what?

(USER translates some more. Presses fire button again. Icon disappears. USER tries to call it back; useless. Screen goes blank.)

USER: Aw nuts!

(USER angrily shuts off COMMODORE.)

COMMODORE: Load"PRG",8,1

USER: This is the LAST time.

COMMODORE: File not found.

USER: *!!h43!!# ! What happened?

(USER finds manufacturer's long distance number on the back of software box and dials it. A machine in an unknown tongue gives message. USER records message, hangs up, then translates.)

USER: Sorry, sucker! We're out of business! But we got your money! PBLLLLITTTTT!

(USER throws disks and package out the window, where a passing parade of

3rd grade acupuncturists stomp all over it. USER reboots COMMODORE with favorite terminal package and calls favorite board.)

COMMODORE: Message #1102. TO: All FROM: Me

Watch out for a program who's docs are written in an unknown tongue. They're bogus and company is out of business. I just got burned.

(USER signs out of that message base and goes to another.)

COMMODORE: Message #887. TO: All FROM: Jester

There were these three guys who went to heaven...

(USER reads joke and laughs so hard he pees his pants. This shorts out power supply and COMMODORE. Screen goes blank.)

USER: Oh, man!

(USER goes to closet and gets down a new set of clothes, another COMMODORE and a power supply. Takes down the broken one and puts up the backup one.)

COMMODORE: Commodore 64 Basic V2 64K Ram System 38911 Basic Bytes Free

USER: (Smiles) I love my Commodore!

THE NEW FAÇADE TO – "ADVERTISEMENT FOR OFF"

Back when I first wrote this piece, I noticed that all the computers on the job I was working at had this crazy screen saver called "the dancing baby." Even though this was cute, it still seemed like a waste of electricity and memory. But also, back then, people were buying desktop computers at $2,500 just to play solitaire on. For that kind of money, a person could hire a kid from the neighborhood to shuffle and deal out a deck of cards on a part time basis.

Anyway, when comparing Commodore to the IBMs of the day, it seemed like I was coming out ahead with my 64K of memory doing what it was designed to do instead of wasting time bogging down the memory with useless things like a screen saver of an infant getting jiggy with it and countless other programs that really seemed to serve no purpose. A simple push of a button and I have activated more than just a screen saver but a power saver as well. I was doing my monitor and my wallet a favor by shutting it off. An idea began to form in my mind on how I would present this new discovery to the world, so I would have to write a great infomercial, one that would bring this idea to the forefront. When this piece was done, I posted it on the bulletin board for all to read on a weekend. When the following Monday came I found half of the monitors in the control office shut off, but the towers were still running. This message reached out to 50% of the people, so I incorporated it into the piece you are about to read.

This was a blast to write as I tried my best to create the infomercial experience for the Commodore. Here it is 10 years later and it is still a hoot. Please enjoy the rewrite.

ADVERTISEMENT FOR OFF

Have you ever been asked this question: WHAT'S YOUR FAVORITE SCREEN SAVER PROGRAM?

How do you answer? Do you confess that you're a Commodore user and Commodore doesn't have a screen saver? Do you lie about the subject? Do you change the subject altogether to something about lingerie for amphibians?

Well now you can hold your head up high, take a deep breath, and say, "My favorite screen saver is OFF."

Yes, now you can own the amazing screen saver for Commodore called OFF. OFF is a universal screen saver that is built directly into your monitor or TV, no matter what make or model it is. No extra memory is required to use OFF. Whenever you wish to walk away from your Commodore for a while and not burn up your screen, just look for the built in switch marked OFF (or POWER on late model monitors and televisions) and press (or turn, depending again on your style of video transmitter) and POOF! Your screen is a complete blank! Blackout! Isn't that amazing? But before you decide to use it, please read some of the most frequently asked questions about OFF:

QUESTION: What is OFF?

ANSWER: OFF is that little switch located on your monitor or television. It allows you to save wear and tear on your video device without any extra memory being accessed.

QUESTION: Why do I need OFF?

ANSWER: OFF is the non-IBM answer to screen savers that allows you to keep your computer on and still retain everything in its memory while making your monitor seem inactive. OFF is the non-IBM user's response to any and all screen saver packages.

QUESTION: Where can I find OFF?

ANSWER: The wonderful thing about OFF is that you already possess it! Just look on your video transmitter for a knob or button marked OFF or POWER and use it.

QUESTION: How much does OFF cost?

ANSWER: OFF comes complete in your set and should cost you nothing extra. Just look for it anywhere on your monitor and begin the savings. OFF compliant sets run anywhere from $10.00 to $10,000.00 and more.

QUESTION: What if my TV or monitor does not have OFF?

ANSWER: If your device does not possess OFF, then take it back to the salvage yard you got it from and demand your money back! All video sets should possess OFF. If your dealer refuses to give you an exchange or refund for your non-OFF compliant set, and you previously signed a purchase agreement stating that your set did not contain OFF, then you've been suckered and deserve the non-OFF compliant set. You can, however, clean out the components and make a lovely planter out of it. Place it in your favorite room and fill it with your most treasured floral arrangement for an uplifting look to any decor.

QUESTION: What must I do to deactivate the OFF option?

ANSWER OFF comes, at no extra charge to you, with the revolutionary device called ON, which is built right into OFF! To deactivate OFF, just press OFF again and surprise! You've disarmed OFF and ON comes into existence (or press POWER on later model units for the same effect). Your screen comes back and you're ready to go have more computing fun!

QUESTION: What are the advantages of OFF?

ANSWER: Some of the advantages of OFF are:

1) Saves computer memory --

OFF uses exactly zero computer memory since everything it takes to run OFF is built directly into the monitor or television.

2) Saves video screen burn --

When you use OFF, you kill the power that goes to the monitor, thus any video feed coming from your computer is stopped at the video ports, thus again saving your cathode-ray tube from any unnecessary wear.

3) Saves electricity --

One of OFF's greatest advantages is to your wallet. When OFF is activated, the electrical flow is stopped. When this flow has ceased, money goes from the power company to your bank account. Talk about a reverse transaction! When you start using OFF, compare your last electrical bill before OFF with your bill after OFF and pocket the difference. With that kind of savings you'll be able to proudly tell the kids, "Yes, you can have that super sized!"

QUESTION: What are the disadvantages of OFF?

ANSWER: So far our researchers have found only one drawback. In the case of various makes and models of video transmitters, and the process of using OFF's unique double capability of ON, it may take anywhere from five seconds to five minutes for an image to appear. But compare this drawback to the advantages -- well, you do the math -- 3-1=2! -- That's two! Double the pluses! Twice the benefit! A twofold reason to use OFF!

QUESTION: Will OFF work with other computers besides Commodore?

ANSWER: Our researchers again have found that so far, OFF will work with any computer system or gaming console. So whether you use a Commodore 64 or a Nintendo 64, OFF will shut down the monitor or television and leave the memory of the system intact.

QUESTION: I've been using OFF for some time and found that OFF is on my keyboard, drive, and some other peripherals. I've even found OFF on the walls, microwave, and other places in my home; if OFF is such a new thing, how come I find it everywhere?

ANSWER: We never claimed OFF was new. In fact, OFF's use was first recorded as far back as the twelfth century A.D., in the vernacular that we are using it in this context. OFF has always existed even on the first video transmitters. We are just bringing public awareness back to that simple switch and encourage all to save product wear and money by using it.

QUESTION: What if I accidently flip the OFF switch on my computer instead of the monitor?

ANSWER: If your data in the keyboard is saved on disk or hard drive, you can deactivate OFF on the computer itself, reboot, reload, and you're back in business. If you didn't save the data, you're shafted pal.

QUESTION: Then should I not use OFF?

ANSWER: Use some common sense and pay attention when using OFF! Sheesh, what a moron!

QUESTION: Do you have to be so insulting?

ANSWER: Do you have to be such an imbecile?

QUESTION: I don't have to stand here and take this abuse!

ANSWER: You can stand, walk, jog, or run, either way you're still a schmuck!

And there you have it! The arguments and subsequent mudslinging generated by OFF! Now don't you feel more like a politician?

Remember, the use of OFF is up to you but you now don't have to feel the pressure from all those nincompoop IBM users who think wasting memory, monitor, and electricity is cool. Be smart, use OFF today!

The following Commodore hardware and software was used in the preparation of this book:

Commodore 128 computer; Commodore 1571 disk drive; Commodore 1541 disk drive; Commodore 1581 disk drive; Magnavox RGB monitor; Seikosha SP-1000VC dot matrix printer; GEOS 128 v2.0 operating system; GEOWrite 2.1 word processor; Big Blue Reader 4.0 conversion software; Wrong is Write v8.0 PET to GEOWrite translator software; and various 3.5 and 5.25 disks.

The following PC hardware and software was used in the preparation of this book:

Compaq Presario C500 laptop computer; Datastation 3.5 external drive; various flashdrives; Vista OS; and Microsoft Word 2007 word processor.

BIBLIOGRAPHY

"The Most Destructive Baby in the Commodore Universe" was first published in the June 1995 issue of Ryte Bytes and is copyrighted 1995 by the Commodore Users Group of Kansas City. Used with permission.

"In Praise of My Sons" was first published in the May 2000 issue of Ryte Bytes and is copyrighted 2000 by the Commodore Users Group of Kansas City. Used with permission.

"Let's get Down to Basics Again" was first published in the August 1999 issue of Ryte Bytes and is copyrighted 1999 by the Commodore Users Group of Kansas City. Used with permission.

"I'll Never Touch Your Commodore Again!" was first published in the May 1995 issue of Ryte Bytes and is copyrighted 1995 by the Commodore Users Group of Kansas City. Used with permission.

"Add The Following: 3 Cats + 1 Commodore = Trouble!" was first published in the July 1995 issue of Ryte Bytes and is copyrighted 1995 by the Commodore Users Group of Kansas City. Used with permission.

"A View on GEOS" was first published in the February 2000 issue of Ryte Bytes and is copyrighted 2000 by the Commodore Users Group of Kansas City. Used with permission.

"And Now For Something Different" was first published in the August 1995 issue of Ryte Bytes and is copyrighted 1995 by the Commodore Users Group of Kansas City. Used with permission.

"My Fight With CDC" was presented under a different title but the contents was first published in the February, March, and April 1999 issues of Ryte Bytes and is copyrighted 1999 by the Commodore Users Group of Kansas City. Used with permission.

ABOUT THE AUTHOR

Author (left) with children (l. to r.) Robert & Erica, (holding a Commodore C64C), and Gabriel. Photo by Micheal Hernandez.

As an avid user of the old Commodore 64 computer, I have been involved as a programmer, my biggest success being honored in the last issue of RUN magazine with my program "Check It Out" I love using the machine as it still seems to have some spunk left in those old chips. I am president of the Commodore Users Group of Kansas City and newsletter editor. I also serve on the staff of the Fresno Commodore Users Group as newsletter editor. I currently live in Kansas City, Kansas

www.ingramcontent.com/pod-product-compliance
Lightning Source LLC
La Vergne TN
LVHW090008070326
832903LV00065B/8